Discovering the Presence of God
Where You Least Expect It

SURPRISED
BY WORSHIP

TRAVIS COTTRELL

WITH INTRODUCTION BY
BETH MOORE

ZONDERVAN®   A WORTHY BOOK

ZONDERVAN.com/
AUTHORTRACKER
follow your favorite authors

ZONDERVAN

Surprised by Worship
Copyright © 2010 by Travis Cottrell

This title is also available as a Zondervan ebook.
Visit www.zondervan.com/ebooks.

This title is also available in a Zondervan audio edition.
Visit www.zondervan.fm.

Requests for information should be addressed to:

Zondervan, *Grand Rapids, Michigan* 49530

Library of Congress Cataloging-in-Publication Data

Cottrell, Travis.
   Surprised by worship : discovering the presence of God where you least expect it /
Travis Cottrell ; with an Introduction by Beth Moore.
      p. cm.
   ISBN 978-0-310-33035-6 (hardcover, jacketed)
   1. God (Christianity)—Worship and love. 2. Christian life. I. Title.
BV4817.C68 2010
248.3—dc22   2010029170

Packaged by Worthy Media. For subsidiary and foreign language rights, contact info@worthymedia
.com.

Cover design: Christopher Tobias
Cover photography: Colin Anderson, Getty Images
Interior design: Susan Browne

Printed in the United States of America

10 11 12 13 14 15 16 17 18 /DCI/ 23 22 21 19 18 17 16 15 14 13 12 11 10 9 8 7 6 5 4 3 2 1

This book is dedicated to my bride, Angela—

who always has ears to hear the voice of God,

eyes to see the works of God,

and a heart to chase after the things of God.

May God surprise you with countless wonderful

altars from which to worship Him.

CONTENTS

Surprising Things I've Learned about Worship:
An Introduction by Beth Moore 7

1. Surprises 27

2. I Got Chills, They're Multiplyin' 41

3. Not Without Hope 52

4. The Sweet, Sweet Sound of Worship 63

5. The Wide, Wide World of Worship 78

6. Words, Wounds, and Worship 87

7. Fear. Not. 103

8. The Great Adventure 114

9. Surviving Death 133

10. Surrender 147

SURPRISING THINGS I'VE LEARNED ABOUT WORSHIP

An Introduction by
Beth Moore

I couldn't be happier to contribute an introduction to this book because it connects me with two subjects that are very dear to my heart: worship and Travis Cottrell. I guess you could say the two subjects are often wrapped up in one bundle for me, because so much of my experience with Travis involves worship. As we've partnered together for thirteen years and more events than either of us could count, I can tell you that Travis is exactly the man he seems to be when he's on the platform. He has one of the most remarkable, God-given gifts to inspire people to lift their hearts to God that I have ever seen. I have been enormously blessed by sharing amazing worship moments with him where God has moved with astonishing power and presence in the lives of thousands of people.

As you will see in this book, another thing Travis and I have in common are those profound moments that come when a person is surprised by some unexpected act or provision of God—when a prayer is dramatically answered; when an unexpected peace bathes you in a time of trouble; when God takes you by the hand and leads you in an unexpected direction; or when you ask for a mere loaf of bread and God gives you a bakery!

I don't know why we keep on being surprised at the blessings God pours out in our moments of worship, whether public or private. It happens enough that you'd think I would start taking those blessings in stride and yawn a *ho-hum* out of sheer familiarity. But like a kid who delights when Dad repeats the same bedtime story night after night, I can't help but thrill when God keeps on surprising me, no matter how often it happens. All I can do in response is to lift my hands or fall on my knees and worship.

This idea of surprise in worship has been on my heart for a long time: what is there about lifting our hearts to God that triggers such unexpected blessings? That is why I am so happy that Travis has written this book. I don't know of anyone more qualified to address that divine serendipity than Travis Cottrell, both by his ability to bring people closer to God in worship and, even more, by his own personal experiences with God's resulting surprises.

Before you plunge into the insights my dear friend and co-laborer has in store for you, permit me to switch places with him this time and be used of God—if He'd so grant me the privilege—to open for Travis. Before he comes to bring the message, I'd like to offer you three insights into worship that, I believe, will prepare you for what Travis has to say.

WORSHIP CAN MAKE
THE EARTH SHAKE

Paul and Silas don't see it coming. They are just going about the streets of Philippi, preaching, healing, and casting out demons, when suddenly they find themselves before the authorities for disturbing the peace. The magistrates order them to be stripped and beaten, and the crowd eagerly joins in. Paul and Silas's skin is torn apart by the severe flogging—and when the Word of God uses the word *severe* for a flogging, it means they were beaten half to death. After the beating they are thrown into prison, and the jailer is commanded to guard them carefully. He locks them in an inner cell and fastens their feet in the stocks.

At about midnight Paul and Silas fall into prayer and begin singing hymns to God. Other prisoners listen, at first out of curiosity, then awe. Suddenly there is such a violent earthquake that the foundations of the prison are shaken. At once all the prison doors fly open, and everyone's chains come loose.

See what can happen when we worship? Talk about a worship surprise! It can shake the very earth.

I would suggest to you that Paul and Silas did not really feel much like worshiping that night. They did it by a conscious choice, and in that moment they overcame every power of darkness. As I read this account from the book of Acts, it occurred to me that there is so much purification in persecution. You see, when we don't have a negative force coming against us to unspoil us and unify us, then we struggle to worship because in the good times we tend to center on ourselves instead of God. We don't like that song the worship leader chose. The drums are too loud. Or we can't believe the worship leader would wear wrinkled jeans and flip-flops and leave his shirt hanging out.

You know what I'm talking about, don't you? You know those times when you're not going to sing because you are not in the mood? Somehow things aren't just right for you, so you sit there with your mouth closed . . . and your heart.

But then I am shamed when I suddenly remember a couple of guys locked deep in a dark dungeon, clamped in chains and torn to shreds, who lifted up their voices in the midst of so much pain. Sometimes you praise first and you feel it later. Yes, you read that right. You just praise God even when you don't feel like it, and then you almost always find that the feeling will come. I'm not saying that the earth will always shake, but I think it will always at least quiver a little. I am convinced that if you lay self aside and focus on God, you will experience a blessing.

My guess is that when that earthquake came as Paul and Silas were singing, they didn't immediately see it as a blessing. Earthquakes are devastating and scary, and we don't want any part of them. They tear up things. But I am convinced that earthquakes can at times be the best things that ever happen to us.

Earthquakes occur in our personal lives, in our marriages, with our kids, in our careers, and in our businesses. Violent earthquakes. And when we experience such devastation, our feelings are not positive at all. Our world may be torn apart—our homes, our relationships, our health, or our finances—spawning all sorts of downer feelings such as grief, confusion, anger, embarrassment, or shame. With such negative feelings roiling about in our souls, the temptation is often to avoid worship experiences—corporately or personally. Just run away and hide. We do this because we don't understand what God knows: that sometimes it takes a violent earthquake to bring us to Him.

We can find, even as the ground shakes, that God is working all things together for good. That's what Paul and Silas discovered. No doubt the first thing they noticed was that their stocks were broken loose and the prison doors were shattered. They could escape! But instead of bolting for the door, they stayed and focused on God. And because they held fast to Him, there was a greater and more blessed surprise coming. When the panicking jailer found that all his prisoners were present, he opened his heart to God, along with his entire family. Paul and Silas were set free.

God uses earthquakes in your life and in my life—those unexpected, violent moments that come to us—so we will see, as Hebrews tells us, exactly "what cannot be shaken" (12:27). When things begin to shake, and we hold fast to that which cannot be shaken and praise the Lord anyway, those bonds that have enslaved us will begin to drop away.

People are not looking for you to have it all together; people are looking at what happens to you when you don't. How do you respond when the earthquake comes? When others see you focus on God and worship, and they watch your bonds fall free, they too will come to recognize the unshakable and cling to Him in their own earthquakes.

So you see, what happens in worship does not stay in worship. We live it out; others witness it, and they are changed.

WORSHIP OUT OF YOUR NEED

I feel pretty sure that when Paul and Silas sang in prison that night, they didn't put on an act in front of the other prisoners, pretending that everything was hunky-dory. Sometimes we approach worship as if we have to feel something we just do not feel. It may surprise you to learn that this is the very opposite of what we must do when we approach God. We are told to "worship Him . . . in spirit and truth" (John 4:24 NKJV). Truth means not posing, not acting like we feel something we don't. Like Paul and Silas, we don't wait for the good feelings; we worship God when it hurts.

Hebrews 4:15–16 says, "For we do not have a high priest who is unable to sympathize with our weaknesses, but we have one who has been tempted in every way, just as we are—yet was without sin. Let us then approach the throne of grace with confidence, so that we may receive mercy and find grace to help us in our time of need."

You see, we can approach God honestly, exposing our warts and all, because we have a God who has been where we are. He too was beaten to a pulp. He had moments when He really dreaded going through with what was facing Him (remember Gethsemane). Before time began, God purposed that He would wrap His one and only Son in a garment of flesh and send Him earthward to dwell among us and take on our terrestrial estate. In the most profound sense, He came to break the laws of nature. Our fallen nature.

In those times when we resist true worship because we don't feel true—when we are afraid to expose our true feelings—we must remember the name of Jesus, the One who understands our fallenness and who came to lift us up. There is no name like Jesus.

I wonder where this moment finds you. Maybe someone has really hurt you, or you've been recently betrayed or rejected. Maybe you're angry, confused, full of doubt, questioning everything you've believed, afflicted in a stronghold of sin. Believe me, I know what that's like. On the other hand, perhaps you're elated—just bursting with songs of praise.

Wherever this moment finds you, the essence of all true worship is that each of us comes to worship God in spirit and in truth. That means being honest about what we feel inside. *Lord, I really hurt, and I'm in chains. I don't feel like worshiping right now, but I know that whatever the circumstances, You are all I need.* We may as well be honest with God; we can't fool Him. He looks straight into our hearts. He knows what drives us and what distracts us— what we feel and what we wish we felt—better than we do. Once you get used to this idea, you'll be surprised at how it frees up your worship. Our transparency is our liberty. "You will know the truth, and the truth will set you free" (John 8:32).

The essence of all worship is coming in our true estate as those who need mercy, those who need grace. Mercy to alleviate; grace to equip, to empower, to anoint, to abound. This "coming with our need exposed" is important because God cannot surprise us unless we are willing to receive His blessings when we worship. We've got to come to God in our honest condition. Whatever you're going through, worship Him out of that. Just be true with it.

If you've been afraid to worship God as you are, turn the tables and surprise Him for a change. Bring Him your pain, your chains, your doubts. *Help Thou my unbelief, Lord. You know my questions. You know my disappointments. You know what I am going through. I just want to worship You in truth.*

Let down your guard. Cut the bull. Because that's when the surprise comes. That's where change comes to your life.

Worship out of whatever pains you, concerns you, or absolutely delights you. Enter your worship by being true before God. Sometimes I know I need to do this, but I don't want to. Is it just me, or don't you sometimes feel that way too? *Lord, I need you to heal my "want to" because that's what is really messed up.*

Are you one who could use a little mercy, a little grace? Do you have a longing that has not been met? Me too. The thing to do is fall down and worship. There is still a mercy seat. It was never God's intention that we would come bringing our all and receive nothing in return. We come to worship to pour it out, in order to make room for Him to pour it in. To pour in the surprise.

What is your need? Worship Him out of that space.

WHAT DO YOU SEE WHEN
YOU WORSHIP?

We are sometimes surprised by a worship experience that is totally unexpected. That's what happened big-time to three of Christ's own disciples. Matthew 17 says: "After six days Jesus took with him Peter, James and John the brother of James, and led them up a high mountain by themselves. There he was transfigured before them. His face shone like the sun, and his clothes became as white as the light. Just then there appeared before them Moses and Elijah, talking with Jesus" (vv. 1–3). Talk about a surprise!

For that moment, as Jesus was apart with His disciples on that high mountain, He dropped the guard of His humanity, dropped down His flesh, and stood there before them in His unveiled God-ness. Those gaping disciples did not know what to do with what they saw. Then came the second surprise. Suddenly Moses and Elijah appeared with Jesus. What a strange thing! Luke tells us that they began talking to Jesus about His departure. The word *departure* in the Greek is the word from which we get *exodus*. Elijah and Moses were talking to Jesus about His own exodus. Do you see the connection? What the transfigured men had in common were their strange departures from Planet Earth.

Then "Peter said to Jesus, 'Lord, it is good for us to be here. If you wish, I will put up three shelters—one for you, one for Moses and one for Elijah'" (v. 4). Now, mind you, while growing up as a Jewish boy, Peter has heard stories about these great men all his life. Somehow he has a knowing upon him that this is Elijah and Moses talking with Jesus, and he has something to say . . . instead of listening. "I'm going to put up three structures and we'll stay here. We are going to have our own little feast of tabernacles right here in this place."

One of my daughters, who will remain unnamed in case she happens to read this, grew up with her mother's propensity for talking in class. When she was in the sixth grade I got a note from her teacher, saying, "The problem is, she's such a brilliant child; but I need her to let me teach some." So I had a word with the vocal little genius about talking when she has not been asked to talk. She replied, "But Mom, why be quiet when you can talk?"

Profound, wasn't it?

That was Peter's philosophy. And the Bible says that at this very moment while he was still speaking—that means while Peter's motormouth was still running—"a bright cloud enveloped them, and a voice from the cloud said, 'This is my Son, whom I love; with him I am well pleased. Listen to him!'" (v. 5). Paraphrase: "Shut thee up!" Listen, Peter; *listen*.

Peter and the others had just had a Sinai experience. That, of course, is something Moses knew all about. Exodus 19 says that Moses was invited to ascend to the top of the mountain and—I'm using the exact terminology—God *descended* to the top of the mountain (v. 18). No matter how high you and I climb on this planet, our God has to descend to get there. You see, there ain't no high like the Most High! Listen to Him!

I love the interchange on that mountain between God and those three disciples about His Son. You see, we gain security from the Word of God if we go to it and see what God says about His own beloved Son. "This is My Son. I am really crazy about Him. Listen to what He has to say. I am well pleased." Matthew then tells us: "When the disciples heard this, they fell facedown to the ground, terrified. But Jesus came and touched them. 'Get up,' he said. 'Don't be afraid.' When they looked up, they saw no one except Jesus" (vv. 6–8).

Pause for a moment and let that phrase sink in: "They saw no one except Jesus." We will know that we have truly worshiped if, when we get up from that place, there is nobody in our spiritual vision but Jesus Himself. That is what made the worship of Paul and Silas so meaningful. That's why pain, chains, devastating relationships, betrayals, and disappointment with others can lead to an unparalleled worship experience in your personal life. If you admit your pain, you worship, and then you just listen, God can give you the surprise. If you come out of any worship experience and see nobody lifted up but Jesus, then you will find your own heart lifted and your spirit in peace. That is a surprise that worship can give if we listen only to Jesus.

WHOSE SONG ARE YOU SINGING?

There are many ways to worship God, but one of the most obvious and meaningful is through singing. That's how

Paul and Silas worshiped, and that, of course, is Travis Cottrell's forte. Not only can that man sing, he has a special gift for inspiring others to lift their voices in praise.

Paul affirms singing as a means of worship, telling us that we are called to worship in psalms, hymns, and spiritual songs (Eph. 5:19). As Paul notes, there is more than one kind of song through which we can express our worship. In fact, there are many kinds. They vary in their tone and tempo, and even in their temporal expression. Some inspire us to feel awe. Others convict us deeply—perhaps even causing us to mourn over sin. Many songs inspire us to shout and dance and clap our hands just like the psalmist. There are also songs of proclamation such as "Our God Saves" and "There Is No One Like Jehovah." There are songs of declaration that say things like, "If God is on our side, who can be against us?" and "I am my Beloved's, and He is mine."

But no song of praise is likely to move us more than the one that we can make our own—one that seems to tell our own story with God. Nothing incites our truest worship like living the lyric, "I will sing of my Redeemer."

No one can sing of your Redeemer for you. No one can tell your story for you. Not like you can. God is listening for your very voice, lifted in praise, singing the song that tells your own story. Even if you think your attempts at singing produce nothing but a croak, then croak with all your heart. He delights when you bring to Him a joyful noise, even if you think it's just a noise. The ultimate purpose of all praise is not to display our melodic windpipes but to exalt our God.

Revelation 14 paints a vivid picture of worship around the throne of God. It tells us that His name is written on the worshipers' foreheads, and that they sing what Scripture says is a new song. But here is the most intriguing part. Verse 3 tells us that no one could learn the song of the redeemed *except the redeemed*. You see, we can sing the words to a song but we can't really *learn* that song from the depths of our soul until we have lived that lyric. Until we feel the truth of what we sing at the center of our heart. That's what raises our voices. That's what sweeps our souls upward.

C. S. Lewis knew firsthand the kind of surprises God

gives to those who turn to Him. His own autobiography was titled *Surprised by Joy*, and in another book he had this to say about the unexpected joy we receive simply by worshiping:

> . . . we must suppose ourselves to be in perfect love with God—drunk with, drowned in, dissolved by that delight which, far from remaining pent up within ourselves as incommunicable . . . bliss, flows out from us incessantly again in effortless and perfect expression, our joy no more separable from the praise in which it liberates and utters itself than the brightness a mirror receives is separable from the brightness it sheds.[1]

If we get no more surprise from worship than this joy that unexpectedly washes over us in releasing our own song from our hearts—our overflowing praise to the God we love dearly—that, for me, is surprise enough. But as Travis will show you in this book, God loves to give even

---

[1] C. S. Lewis, *Reflections on the Psalms* (New York: Harcourt Brace, 1958), p. 96.

more. He loves to give the unexpected. He loves to add surprise upon surprise to those who love Him. To see what I mean, I urge you to continue reading this book. I think you'll be surprised. Happily surprised.

With great joy, I now hand you over to the servant whose book you picked up and whose message you want to hear. Please relish your time with my dear co-laborer and beloved son in the faith, Travis Cottrell. You're going to love him.

1

SURPRISES

surprise (**v.**) *to be caught unawares; to experience wonder,*
amazement, or shock at the unexpected

I've been thinking a lot lately about surprises.

My wife recently threw me a surprise party for my . . .
uh, well . . . let's just say it was a *significant* birthday. And I
have to admit, she completely got me; I had no idea what
was coming. In fact, hindsight has shown me how clueless
I really was. Looking back, I can't see how I missed all the
slips, all the hints that were dropped. But miss them I did.
Even up to the final moments, as I approached the door
that separated me from so many of my friends dressed in
horrible '80s garb, I had no idea what I was about to walk
into.

Why was I not suspicious when, on a night three days

before my birthday, my wife had us driving out to a random building in the middle of a snowstorm? Why wasn't I suspicious that this woman—who never looks anything less than perfect—chose to leave home on this night with teased-out hair that would've rivaled Loretta Lynn, circa 1981? (Seriously, if that Rave hair spray didn't turn me on to what was happening, you may wonder whether I may be too oblivious to even notice when the Lord returns!)

In any case, she got me. She and my friends *all* got me. The warnings whizzed over my head, and I was blindsided. And you know what? I loved it. I loved every minute of it.

VARIED SURPRISES

The joy of the surprise really overwhelmed me. I could hardly believe that so much time and energy went into something that was just for me. All of the planning, all of these dear people coming together—it made my heart leap. It made me feel loved. It was a moment in time that made me feel special. It was my favorite kind of surprise.

But there are other kinds of surprises that I don't like so much.

I will never forget the call that came one day when I was in the studio rehearsing with some singers. We were in the middle of some good, intense work on a song for a CD when the phone rang. It was my wife, Angela, telling me that our youngest boy had been in an accident. Little Levi, who was just one year old at the time, had been hurt while playing on a trampoline. A blow on the neck had left him unable to move, and she was rushing him to the emergency room. I left immediately and broke all kinds of traffic laws heading to the hospital.

The unwanted surprise. It's the kind of surprise that no one looks forward to, that everyone hates. Yet it's the kind that eventually comes to us all. The scenarios are different and the outcomes vary, but we are never ready for the unwanted surprise.

There's another kind of surprise that I absolutely cannot stand: *the surprise you know is coming* (a.k.a., *the anticipated surprise*). "Okay, so if you know it's coming, then how can it be a surprise?" you ask. But you know what I mean. It's the friend who calls and says, "I need to talk to you about something important"—and then follows up with, "Can we meet next week?" It's the mailing of the résumé or the college application—and then watching the mailbox for the result. It's the visit to the doctor who runs you through all kinds of tests involving needles, probes into unmentionable places, and noisy, cold-slabbed, claustrophobic machines—only to conclude, "We'll analyze the results and call you next Friday."

More often than not, the news we have been waiting for is not what gets us. It's the *waiting* that nearly does us in. The tension of waiting for the arrival of the unknown is nerve-wracking. Almost unbearable. It's the nature of the anticipated surprise. Don't even come near me with it!

Nevertheless, as I step back and look at what I've learned about God from His Word, and from what He has allowed to come to pass in my own life, I see this: God is into surprises. Huge, life-altering surprises. Small, gentle surprises. Surprises that come out of nowhere. Surprises that we anticipate but must wait for.

Sometimes God even shows Himself in unwanted surprises.

UPSIDE-DOWN BELIEF

I find it interesting that we tend to base our beliefs regarding God's goodness and love on the nature of the surprises He gives us. As long as His surprises are happy ones like birthday parties, we remain confident and secure: *He really is good! He evidently loves me a lot!* But all too often unwanted surprises have a way of turning our theology upside down.

Think of those million or so Hebrew slaves that Moses led out of Egypt. As they leave their cruel masters, they are elated. God has really done a job for them. He has given the Egyptians their comeuppance for all those centuries of eighty-hour weeks with no overtime pay, benefits, or raises; no wages, even! Now God's people are headed for a country He has reserved for them. A country where they will be the landholders and overlords. And they haven't had to lift a finger. It's all a gift. God did all the work, and all they will have to do is march into that rich land and settle in. God is really good. He is truly a God of love.

But suddenly everything changes. They are barely out of Goshen when, coming up behind them, they hear the ominous sounds of an unwanted surprise—the hoofbeats of warhorses and the clatter of chariot wheels. The Egyptian army! And there's no way to escape because Moses has led them right up to the banks of the Red Sea. Surely all is lost. They are caught in a seemingly inescapable trap between an advancing army and an engulfing body of water. How could God have done this? If He really loved them, why would He allow such a thing to happen? This was the big one . . . the big game. How could Moses throw the big one?

But just as the people are ready to rebel and return to slavery, God has Moses lift his staff over the sea—and then comes a really big surprise. The water gathers itself up into two opposing walls, forming an aisle of dry land leading all the way to the far shore.

Those wide-eyed masses don't wait for a red carpet to roll out. Mysteriously, the walls of water inspire them to shut their grumbling mouths. They scurry across to the safety of the Sinai peninsula while God holds back the Egyptian army with a massive tower of fire. When all the Hebrews reach the far shore, God extinguishes the fire and Pharaoh's finest charge into the liquid-walled corridor.

When the entire Egyptian army is running like mad across
the seabed, those walls suddenly collapse, turning the army
into fish food. And suddenly God is good again.

The Bible tells us that now everyone "put their trust
in him and in Moses his servant" (Exod. 14:31). In fact,
Moses and the people burst into a praise song right there
on the shore:

> The LORD is my strength and my song;
> he has given me victory.
> This is my God, and I will praise him—
> my father's God, and I will exalt him!
> (Exod. 15:2 NLT)

Well, YEAH! Who wouldn't praise God after what He
had just done? But read on in Exodus and you'll see that
the Israelites' praise was constantly off and on, depending
on what the Lord had done for them lately. When the good
surprises came, they exalted Him. When the unwanted
surprises came, they whined and complained and threat-
ened to head back to the Egyptian sweatshop.

Still, I need to be careful about judging these fickle people, because I'm afraid I may be more like them than I want to admit.

FACING UNCERTAIN ENDINGS

As I sped to the hospital that day, tears streamed down my face as I cried out to God for my little boy to be okay. I begged for mercy over his sweet life. I began to recount the things God says about Levi—that he is fearfully and wonderfully made . . . that Jesus came to give him life, and life more abundantly . . . that if God is for him, no one can be against him. I reminded God of one great and precious promise after another.

After just a few minutes of driving, my phone rang. It was Angela. My heart stopped, waiting for her to speak.

"Turn around," she said.

"Why? What's going on?"

"Levi is fine. Something has happened—he's now wide-awake and moving freely. I'm taking him on in to have him checked out, just to be sure, but his mobility and alertness are back."

I pulled the car over to the shoulder of the narrow road and wept. My heart was so overwhelmed with relief and gratitude, I didn't know what to do but cry. I was so thankful that the ending to the story was not what it could have been. So thankful that the surprises we sometimes fear will reach our little ones were held at bay this time around. God had done for me what He did for the escaping Hebrews: He had followed an unwanted surprise with a wonderful surprise. God was good.

But what if that second surprise had not been a favorable one? What if—I can hardly bear even to think this, much less write it—my dear little Levi had been brain-damaged, permanently paralyzed, or even killed? Would I still call God "good"? Would I still trust Him? Consider Him worthy of my praise?

Not long after the Hebrews left the Red Sea and marched on to the holy mountain, God called Moses up to its summit to give him the Law. When God descended to meet Moses, smoke surrounded the mountain, and thunder and lightning exploded from it. When the people saw this pyrotechnic display, "they trembled with fear. They stayed at a distance and said to Moses, 'Speak to us yourself and we will listen. But do not have God speak to us or we will die'" (Exod. 20:18–19).

They wanted God as long as He was safe. They wanted the good surprises, but if there was any discomfort involved, then let Him keep His distance, please. "Moses, you go on up there and learn all you want about God, then come back down and give us a filtered, sanitized version of what we need to know. If He has bigger, more complex purposes for us that cause us fear, uncertainty, or—God forbid—actual pain, we don't want to hear about them."

Does any of this sound familiar? (I confess, I can certainly relate!) Insecurity often keeps us from learning more about God. We fear anything about His character or nature that extends beyond our traditional paradigms. That God would have something about Him we have not experienced . . . that He would wrap the surprise we need for our own good within the smoke and thunder of an unwanted surprise . . . that He would move in a way we didn't expect or show Himself in a scenario we would have orchestrated differently . . . bows us up and makes us resistant.

Admittedly, God doesn't always choose to reveal the "why" of our unwanted surprises. But are we going to reject His gifts just because we don't like the brown-paper-and-duct-tape package they're wrapped in? God knows that if we remove the wrapping—if we work through the unwanted part of the surprise and discover the gift inside—we will learn something of His goodness and character that we might not have seen otherwise. Something that can motivate our praise beyond our circumstances the next time an unwelcome surprise comes calling.

Sometimes we take the good for granted—expecting it, claiming it as a right—unless we are forced to see it contrasted with the alternative. With Levi's accident, I had seen the alternative. My sweet boy could have been damaged for life or even lost to me. But instead, God gave me the happy surprise of his fully restored health.

On that particular day, I did not learn whether my commitment to God is strong enough to keep on praising Him through real pain and loss. The harder lesson may come another day though, and I pray that I will steadfastly love Him through it. Like Job, I want my love for God to be such that I will always say, "Though He slay me, yet will I trust Him" (Job 13:15 NKJV) amid every kind of surprise—the happy ones, the anticipated ones, and even the unwanted ones.

NO MATTER WHAT

As I walked back down the corridor to the studio where I had left my singing friends, I heard a sound coming from beyond the door. I paused and listened. They were worshiping. They weren't just singing; they were pursuing God passionately in intercession on behalf of my little boy. I'm telling you, they were going after it—literally dripping with sweat from their worship time. The place was no longer a studio; it was a sanctuary. An altar.

As I listened through the door, I'll never forget the words they were singing:

No guilt in life, no fear in death
This is the power of Christ in me
From life's first cry to final breath
Jesus commands my destiny

No pow'r of hell, no scheme of man
Can ever pluck me from His hand
'Til He returns, or calls me home
Here in the pow'r of Christ I'll stand.[1]

By no means are the endings to our surprise stories always the same. Sometimes the resolution, the healing, or the restoration comes instantly. Sometimes it comes on the other side of this life. So what can we know for sure about God's surprises?

We can know that those surprises are always *for* us, never against us. The surprises may come out of the blue. They may lie just ahead but beyond plain sight. They may be painfully unwanted but desperately needed. Whatever they are and however they come, we can be sure that the Lord God, in His goodness, knows what He is doing.

It helps to remember that nothing is ever a surprise to Him. He is in full control. Knowing this gives us true peace in all circumstances. Be it His perfect or permissive will (or

---

[1] "In Christ Alone." Words and music by Keith Getty and Stuart Townend. © 2002 Thankyou Music (admin. worldwide by worshiptogether.com except for the UK and Europe, which is admin. by Kingsway Music)/PRS.

whatever you may call it), He can be trusted with our lives. That is never a surprise. It is an ongoing, unchanging fact.

As we walk through the doors of surprise along our life's journeys, I find that we can let our frail selves stumble upon the altar of worship, assured that the Lord can be found on every path. Sometimes the most breathtaking surprises are mysteriously sublime, like the beauty of worship in the most unexpected of places.

I want to find the Lord, submit to Him. I long to worship Him, even in the places where I wasn't looking for Him. Even in the places where I never wanted to be.

I know He will meet me there. He will meet you there too.

2

I GOT CHILLS, THEY'RE MULTIPLYIN'

joy (n.) *the expression of delight, rejoicing, or other positive emotion at an accomplishment or the satisfaction of a desire*

I got up at 4:00 a.m. on that Sunday morning and headed for a church just outside of Knoxville. The event was the church's homecoming—their 150th anniversary—and I was participating in a reunion of sorts with some friends I had traveled and sung with years ago.

We were planning to surprise our group's leader, who had been in ministry for many years. Little did I know that on this trip I was going to get a fine surprise myself.

The previous night I'd told my kids that at least two of them had to ride with me. Immediately, Jack and Lily Kate wanted to go; Levi wanted to stay home and go to our church with Angela.

It's still not clear to me why the two older ones jumped so quickly at the chance of riding three hours in a car, sitting through a long church service, and then riding three hours back. But I have a suspicion: I think maybe they figured on exploiting my weakness. They've learned that I will invariably give in to their persistent requests for all manner of snacks and treats. Maybe sometimes a pack of Gummi Bears is worth that much to a kid, I don't know. But whatever "confectionous" motivations may have prodded them, I was happy to have them with me.

The kids slept for the first hour or so of the trip. When they awoke, I decided it was time for some worship music. It was a beautiful morning, and my heart was really tender to the Lord. I had already experienced an amazing weekend at *Living Proof Live—Memphis*, one of my favorite conference events ever. So I was primed to worship. I powered up the iPod, plugged it into the car's sound system, and musically headed where I always go when I'm ready to fire up for worship: Kirk Franklin.

The kids and I sang and bounced and laughed and got our groove on. Then, midway through a song called "Hero,"

I had one of those moments. "Oooh . . . this song gives me chills," I said out loud. I gestured to my arm to show my son: sure enough, the hairs were standing straight up.

Jack had heard me say this before. He's seen me lose it over a song, a sad scene in a movie, even a TV commercial, for crying out loud. So he's used to my expressivism. But after a moment of staring out his window as if recalling some deeply embedded memory, he replied: "I've only gotten chills once before while listening to music."

What? My son had gotten chills? This captured my attention, and I waited for him to tell me more.

I am convinced that when worship music gives us chill bumps, they're a display of the joy we feel when the Holy Spirit moves within us. I know that according to human physiology, chill bumps are formed when tiny muscles connected to hair follicles raise the skin around each hair, causing it to stand up. I don't understand the connection between this physical reaction and emotion in worship, but I see chill bumps as a strong indication of God's spiritual presence.

BEYOND WORDS

I was really curious to know the occasion that gave my son his first chill bumps—what song might have moved him, and whether he understood that the Holy Spirit was speaking to his heart. But Jack didn't say anything more. I bit my tongue and didn't probe. He seemed to be in deep thought and, knowing that parents can sometimes dig too hard when their kids are thinking things through, I didn't want to derail him. So I let it go. But his comment got me thinking about praise music and chill bumps.

It's a strange phenomenon, isn't it? You'd be surprised at how many people never experience chills—except maybe when they come down with the flu. Music doesn't do for them what it does for me and for so many others.

People are often suspicious of what they call "emotionalism" in worship. As the thinking goes, we expressive types mistake emotions for spirituality. By expecting a reaction to the songs, we are mistaking a cheap emotional thrill for a true relationship with God. To make their case, they point to the apostle Paul, who they believe was putting a damper on emotionalism when he said, "I will sing with my spirit, but I will also sing with my mind" (1 Cor. 14:15).

Okay, I'll agree that in some venues, emotions are properly suspect. Our feelings should not guide us in our search for truth. Feelings can be misleading, and when we place them above sound judgment, trouble is likely to follow. That's exactly why so many marriages fail. The tingly, giddy feeling of falling in love often trumps discretion about what makes for lifelong compatibility with a mate. When parents think "the loving thing to do" is to refrain from punishing their little "bundle of joy" for kicking the dog, they're allowing emotions to trump not only good judgment but also God's Word.

Well, now, if there is danger in leaning too heavily on our emotions for a worship response—and I believe there is—just what was King David doing when his joy exploded into a wild dance before the ark of the covenant?

You remember the story. After a long absence, the ark was finally being brought to its proper home in the tabernacle in Jerusalem. David was so elated over the ark's homecoming that he had the Levites lead the people in a joyous worship song. As the celebration began and the ark came into view, the king got so caught up in worship that he stepped down from his high place and danced in the street with wild abandon. Now that's some good ol' emotion right there.

If emotion is so suspect, how do we explain David's compulsion to sing and dance? I think it's really pretty simple. Emotions are suspect *only when we rely on them alone*. They are not to control our actions but to direct our responses.

So Paul's admonition in 1 Corinthians 14 was not a warning against emotion; he was simply saying, "Don't let emotions rule the roost." That rowdy Corinthian church had let their emotions get out of hand. The result was a madhouse in their assemblies, with everything happening on top of everything else. No one could truly worship because of the utter chaos.

Paul was urging his readers to remember that the mind must be involved. It must lead to the truth of God. And when we submit to that truth and see God's love shining through, emotions will follow and should be expressed.

In fact, I will go as far as to say that emotions *must* follow and *must* be expressed.

Truth and emotions go hand in hand. When our heart's desire is to deeply connect with God, to know and experience Him as He truly is, we can't help but be affected when He responds in a very personal way. Receiving what you've longed for is the very definition of joy!

The Christian philosopher Blaise Pascal must have known this firsthand. He's the one who said that while we must know God through the mind, it is in the heart that we actually experience Him. The mind feeds the heart, and from the heart—the emotions—our joy bubbles up.

The point here is that worship involves the whole person—body, mind, and spirit. We know God with our minds; we experience Him in our spirits; and we express the joy of His presence through our voices and bodies.

It seems strange to me that we talk of those three parts of ourselves as if they were separate and divisible. But they are not. Just as it takes three sides to make a triangle or three different oils to make the canned concoction that stops my doors from squeaking, it takes body, mind, and spirit to make a human. Remove any one of these and you no longer have a person. A corpse or a ghost, perhaps, but not a person. So you see, if we're to worship God as we should, we must get the whole person involved. And by all means, that includes the emotions. Maybe *especially* the emotions, because, as Pascal says, that's where we experience joy.

When a song moves me enough to give me chills, I know that I am experiencing God in my heart. The emotion tells me I am connecting; I am feeling His joy. And the emotion can encourage the body to get involved as well.

For King David that meant dancing. For many people it means raising hands. For some of us it often means chill bumps. Through a variety of means, the Holy Spirit touches us in ways that can't be communicated in mere words.

REMINDERS OF HIS PRESENCE

My heart leapt when my son told me that a song had given him chill bumps. It was a hopeful sign that he may have experienced the Holy Spirit in his life. Yet I desperately wanted to know the whole story.

At about eight o'clock Sunday morning we got to the church, and the reunion of dear friends began. Lots of hugging and lots of laughing. And lots of rehearsing for a service that was to begin in less than an hour. My longtime songwriting partner, David Moffitt, and I shared a chuckle at seeing our sons sharing a hymnal—they hardly knew what a hymnal was. But it was also great watching the next generation worshiping together, just as David and I have for so long. After the rehearsal we just hung out and drank coffee until time for worship. (Often coffee is so good it can give me chill bumps too, but that's another book.)

When the service began, nine of us visiting singers sat in the choir loft with the nine or so regulars. Besides doubling the choir's size, we also added to the church's orchestra with our pianist and bass player. It was a small and sweet fellowship. The service played out just as simply and joyfully as one could wish.

The entire congregation sang a couple of hymns, and our visiting group did a special number for them. Then we filed back into the choir loft to sing the choir special— a very simple arrangement of "Thank You." You know the one; it says: "Thank you for giving to the Lord / I am a life that was changed."[1]

Although the arrangement was simple, it was pure and authentic. As we sang, I felt the Lord moving in my heart with deep feelings of gratitude for everyone who had ever sown a seed into my life in some indefinable way. I was having a "moment."

Since I've heard this particular song about 514 times too many in my life, I was surprised to find it moving me so much that day. But it serves me right. It's when we think we've got God figured out that He astonishes us with the totally unexpected.

In that familiar song made fresh by the Holy Spirit, God was reminding me that He can reach us in any way He chooses—we are never beyond whatever means or message He wants to use! In other words, maybe it's time for us to get over our "sophistication."

Yet He wasn't done with me that day either. He had still another surprise in store.

---

[1] "Thank You." Words and music by Ray Boltz. © 1998 by Gaither Music/ASCAP. All rights reserved. International copyright secured.

As we sang, I glanced down at the front row, where my two kids were intermingled with the Moffitt children. My son's eyes locked on mine. And that's when I got my biggest surprise.

Jack had obviously been waiting for me to look at him. He had that expectant look on his face, and a happy and peaceful grin a mile wide that I won't forget as long as I live. He raised his arm in front of him, almost at face level, pointed to it, and mouthed to me, "Chills! I got chills!"

No frills. No graphics. No monitors or drums or electric guitars. Just people. And the presence of God.

A lump of joy came into my throat so that I could hardly sing. My son had just experienced true joy.

3

NOT WITHOUT
HOPE

hope (v.) *to anticipate a desired outcome; to expect*
something with confidence and trust

By birth, I was given a great honor that few in my generation receive: my father was a World War II veteran—a member of what is called "the Greatest Generation." Both of my parents were a bit older than most when I was born. My dad was forty-five and my mom turned forty when I was five days old. In fact, because of my mother's age and her many health issues, the doctors highly recommended she have an abortion. I am really thankful she didn't listen.

As family history goes, Glenn Cottrell was the younger of two sons born to Lloyd and Lillie Cottrell. A quiet, meek couple, Lloyd and Lillie lived and farmed in the rural outskirts of Boone, North Carolina, a small town nestled in the

Appalachian Mountains. Theirs was what we call a simple life. But I'm sure that to Lloyd and Lillie there was nothing simple about letting Uncle Sam take both of their sons off to war. Glenn's older brother, James, was the first to go. Glenn went later in August 1943, when he turned eighteen and became eligible for the draft.

I don't pretend to have a grid for how it must feel to send a child into the service today, much less to send a child from the backroads of North Carolina into international combat. My reading of history tells me that in that time, attitudes were different. Life was harder, faith was stronger, and people were tougher—they took sacrifice and hardship more stoically. But I can't imagine that it was anything less than excruciating for a mother and father to see two sons leave for one of the worst wars in America's history.

If that was difficult for Lloyd and Lillie Cottrell, things were about to get even worse.

On October 17, 1944, many soldiers in Glenn's company were severely wounded in a fierce battle with the Germans. While crossing the German lines to help a wounded comrade, Glenn was captured. His captors took him first to Munich and then to a concentration camp in Mooseburg, Germany, where he spent eight months as a prisoner of war.

Glenn's parents received word of his capture, but after that initial notification, there was never another report as to his whereabouts or condition. When the war ended, Lloyd and Lillie's older son returned from battle, but Glenn did not. Nor did any further news about him.

His parents, these sweet country folk, had no choice but to continue on with life. Day in and day out they hoped for the best, yet that worst-case scenario lurked in the shadows. After all the months of waiting, I sometimes wonder if they were ever tempted to give up hope and resign themselves to the tragic loss of their son. I am sure it was Lillie's first thought when she woke up in the morning and her last when she lay down at night. How her heart must have ached to raise her head from that pillow every morning and face another day, not knowing whether she would ever see her boy again.

When Glenn left for the war, his mother had given him a New Testament encased in a metal cover. Imagine the faith involved in Lillie handing that New Testament to her son. I can't even send my kids off to camp without some measure of angst. I lie awake thinking of them, praying for them, hoping for them. If I had to send my son into a war with a casualty rate as high as that of World War II, I might be tempted to shake my fist at God. But somehow, I can't imagine Lillie Cottrell ever doing that. Her emotions may have been tattered, but I feel sure that her faith prevented despair.

While in battle, Glenn always carried that Bible in the shirt pocket of his uniform. During his eight months of hard labor as a POW, the guards took his every belonging except for the clothes on his back. He wore them for the duration of his captivity, yet somehow Glenn's captors never discovered that metal-bound New Testament that he kept next to his heart.

Since I'm here to write this story, you know that my dad, Glenn, obviously came home. He was liberated on May 1, 1945. After being released he, along with all the other POWS, was fed, cleaned up, given a medical checkup, and treated for illnesses. On June 17, he arrived back in the United States. But my grandparents knew none of this. In the rural mountains of North Carolina, no one had a phone. And no letter or telegram was sent to them, telling the good news.

Today, the men and women returning from service usually arrive home by plane to the welcoming arms of their loved ones. But back then, soldiers were returned to the States by ship and were left to make their individual journeys home from their port of landing. So it took my dad a long while to thumb his way to North Carolina and then up into the mountains to the small town of Boone. Even after arriving in Boone, he still faced a long walk to his parents' farm. He finally reached the house in the dead of night.

My grandparents' bed was in the living room, and in those days no one kept their doors locked. So on that night, at 3:00 a.m., my dad simply walked into his parents' house . . . alive. Startled, his mom and dad jumped out of bed, truly thinking they were seeing a ghost. But this was no ghost. Their son was alive!

WORSHIPING GOD ANYWAY

Talk about a life-impacting moment . . . I wish I could have been a fly on the wall of that simple white farmhouse.

I've tried to imagine the joy my grandparents must have felt, and it's almost more than my heart can take. What they'd dared to hope and pray for had happened. God's "yes" was standing in the flesh in front of them!

Knowing what I do of them, I can be pretty sure of how they responded. I think they did as the two women named Mary did after Jesus was resurrected.

Just in case you have forgotten the details, let me refresh your memory. These two women were grieving at the death of Jesus. They had seen Him tortured and crucified, then laid in a borrowed tomb. Mary Magdelene owed Jesus a tremendous debt of gratitude because He had delivered her from the bondage of seven demons. The other Mary was the mother of one of Jesus' disciples. Both women loved Jesus and had stood by Him during His crucifixion (Matt. 27:56). They were devastated at His death, and in their grief they determined to anoint His body the morning after the Sabbath.

When these women arrived at the tomb on Sunday morning, they were surprised to see the stone rolled away. Their surprise was even greater when an angel met them and told them that Jesus had risen. He showed them the empty tomb, and the overjoyed women ran to tell the disciples. But they hadn't gone far before Jesus Himself greeted them. Talk about being surprised by joy! So what did these women do? They did what anyone who loves Jesus would naturally have done: "They came to him, clasped his feet and worshiped him" (Matt. 28:9).

THE WAIT FOR ANSWERS

I suspect that somewhere in their hearts, my grandparents probably had already been grieving, resigned to the growing likelihood that they would never see their son again. When my dad walked through their front door that morning, scaring them silly and then embracing them in joy, there is no doubt in my mind as to their response: they thanked and worshiped God.

Many times we are required to wait in anguish without answers. In those moments, the thing we fear most is that God may not come through for us. Or worse, maybe that He *hasn't* come through for us. The moment when we really needed Him has passed; the thing we dreaded, occurred. He missed the opportunity to help, and we were left in want, in grief.

It is in those quiet moments of pain that our faith is called out. That is when we must realize: God is holding us closely, and at some point He will come through in a huge way.

God came through big-time for my grandparents. He brought their son back to them and banished their grief and uncertainty. But not every surprise ends so happily, does it? I have watched friends bear the pain of losing a child, and it breaks my heart. Though I try to empathize, I can't fathom the depth of the hurt they experience.

Yet in the sorrows and griefs I have endured, I've discovered that which many Christians throughout the ages have testified to. Even when our uncertainty is not resolved as we'd like, even when we must face the tragedy we feared, holding to our faith will eventually lead us to a moment when God's presence returns. When His voice whispers in our ear once more. When His light again illumines our path.

That is when we can take all the pain and sorrow and offer it up to God. And that is when worship becomes the most beautiful.

Worship out of pain is deep and rich, for it is offered in true faith—a faith that sincerely believes God is holding us in His heart and weeping with us.

UNSHAKABLE BELIEF

My grandparents could worship God in the midst of their uncertainty, in supposed loss—even amid the long separation from their son—knowing that just as God had raised Lazarus from the dead, He would also raise Glenn from the dead (if not in their lifetimes, at least in eternity). They knew that the Lord would one day raise them from death into life as well. So even if they had been bereft of their son for the rest of their lives, they could have firm confidence that a reunion was coming. And in that confidence was the surest hope of all—a hope capable of surprising every grieving heart.

And you know what? That same confidence, that same surprising hope, can be ours.

God happened to bless my grandparents with a reunion on this side of eternity in 1945. But He will bless us all with it on the other side—on that great day when the dead in Christ arise to be forever with the Lord. That is the most powerful reason I can think of to worship Him, even in our pain.

> What, then, shall we say in response to this? If God is for us, who can be against us? He who did not spare his own Son, but gave him up for us all—how will he not also, along with him, graciously give us all things? . . . For I am convinced that neither death nor life, neither angels nor demons, neither the present nor the future, nor any powers, neither height nor depth, nor anything else in all creation, will be able to separate us from the love of God that is in Christ Jesus our Lord. (Rom. 8:31–32, 38–39)

The trustworthiness of God merits our worship. The faithfulness of God merits our surrender. In every situation.

When our sorrow seems so all-consuming and dense, we still have the certainty that nothing is too difficult for our God (Gen. 18:14). And that includes your sorrowful circumstances.

THE SWEET, SWEET SOUND OF WORSHIP

worship (v.) *to show tremendous honor, reverence, or devotion for one who is considered worthy, especially a divine being*

How old do you have to be to qualify as a Pharisee? Or a legalist? Or an outright religious hypocrite?

I think I might have been one as a kid. Okay, I *was* one as a kid.

I was born into a family of Christians who went to church every time the doors opened. I knew Jesus at an early age. So I must have subconsciously taken that as a sign that I could wear the badge of "Christian" like *The Brady Bunch*'s Peter wore his safety patrol badge.

Many of my beliefs were mere opinions, *at first*. But they were sincere enough to harden into convictions— sincerely legalistic convictions, but sincere nonetheless.

And as I got more and more into music, those opinionated ways naturally flowed into my music life.

I'll never forget one day when I was a young teenager, our church's choir director (that's what we called worship leaders back then) tried something different. And it caught me off guard.

Now before we go on, let me tell you: I wasn't a *normal* teenager. I was a church-music nerd already. An opinionated, church-music nerd. I mean, what is natural about a five-year-old knowing the name *Bill Gaither*? Or a ten-year-old whose favorite song is "On the Jericho Road"? Or a fifteen-year-old guy who wears out Amy Grant tapes instead of Styx or REO Speedwagon? (Well, I did play a little REO now and then. But you get my point.) I was a church-music nerd long before I was even old enough to drive.

So there I was, sitting on the front row where I always sat (aren't you impressed?), waiting for church to start. I was fully expecting things to proceed as they should: call to worship, hymn of praise, welcome and announcements, children's sermon, offertory hymn, offering, choir special, message, hymn of invitation, benediction, lunch. I glanced at the bulletin, and it confirmed my expectations: the congregation would sing at three points in the service, all straight from the hymnal, exactly as it ought to be done.

The choir came in as usual and began to sing the simple strains of the then-new worship song "I Love You, Lord." I liked it. It was nice. Then, after they had sung the chorus, the choir director turned to the congregation and said, "Let's all sing that together."

What? I thought. *This song is not in the hymnal! It isn't even mentioned in the bulletin! How can we do this? Why are we doing this? This feels weird. Let the choir sing; I'm going to sit here and read the bulletin.*

The congregation began singing, each member joining in one by one. The piano and organ eventually dropped out, leaving just the sound of those voices ringing off the white walls and stained glass of that small Baptist church sanctuary.

It was beautiful.

I eventually found myself singing along, and my soul— yes, the soul of an obnoxious, opinionated teenager—was quieted in the presence of the Lord like never before.

I was caught off guard, not only by the change in the worship, but even more by my own response. Worship could be different and still be worship.

Surprise.

A TURNING POINT

As insignificant or even silly as it may seem to you, that morning's worship surprise was a turning point for me—the catalyst for a paradigm shift in my understanding of true corporate worship.

I wasn't looking for such a shift. I didn't think I needed it. I very well may have been too young for it. But it happened. And the change it began in me was so monumental that it carries my calling to this day.

As I think back, I wonder how in the world I could have been so caught up in the form and order of things that I would overlook the movement of the Spirit. It's a movement that can come when we allow our hearts to open to the unexpected. Yet how many times do our confining perceptions of corporate worship hold us back from truly communing with God through music? To broaden the question, how often do those same constrictions bleed into other areas of our beliefs—and our lives?

More often than not, it happens without our even noticing. What we learn in our formative years can easily lock itself into our brains as the template for what is true—when in reality, we may simply be the heirs of a man-made tradition commonly known as "the way things always ought to be." And when the Spirit moves in a different way, some of us promptly dig in our heels, refusing to believe that what we learned *first* might not be the whole picture of God's truth.

Or, our resistance may be more a matter of personal preference than early imprinting. A music style might not be to our taste. We may take issue with the pastor's sermons, not because of the content but because of his Bible-thumping intensity or his laid-back informality. We may resist a biblical principle because of the way it's presented rather than its actual truth.

When truth emerges in unfamiliar or unattractive packages, we are prone to become offended and close off to what God might be doing. Remember how Jesus was rejected when He first preached in His hometown of Nazareth? "'Where did this man get these things?' [his neighbors] asked. 'What's this wisdom that has been given him, that he even does miracles! Isn't this the carpenter? Isn't this Mary's son and the brother of James, Joseph, Judas and Simon? Aren't his sisters here with us?' And they took offense at him" (Mark 6:2–3).

They took offense because the message came in an unexpected way. From an unexpected person.

Offense comes so easily, doesn't it? And it can happen not just to know-it-all teenagers or hometown skeptics. Just ask John the Baptist.

TELLING IT LIKE IT IS

John the Baptist and Jesus knew each other. In fact, they were cousins. John spent his entire life pointing people to Jesus. He is the one who proclaimed, "Behold! The Lamb of God who takes away the sins of the world!" (John 1:29 NKJV). He also baptized Jesus. He was so humbled by the task he could hardly bring himself to do it. Talk about not feeling worthy! How would you react if God on earth asked you to baptize Him? ("Who, me? Baptize *you*? Yeah, right.")

At this point John's thinking was healthy. It was rightly set. John performed the baptism, and Jesus went on His way.

No doubt John had formed a grandiose picture in his mind of what Jesus' kingdom would look like. Meanwhile, he had work to do in anticipation of that kingdom. So as he waited for those expectations about Jesus to be fulfilled, he continued his itchy-robed country ministry, eating his sticky-crunchy meals of locusts and honey and preaching to all who would hear.

If John had lain low and kept quiet, things might have just eased along. But when something needs to be said, men like him don't pull any punches; they tell it like it is. So when he had the gall to haul King Herod over the coals for his immoral marriage to his own sister-in-law, John suddenly found himself sharing a prison cell with rats and roaches. Not the kind of outcome he'd hoped for as one who was preparing the way for the Messiah.

Now, John was no namby-pamby. He was a rugged,

no-frills man's man who could take almost anything that anyone dished out. But I'm pretty sure that the stink of the dungeon and a date with a dinner platter didn't fit his paradigm for the way God's kingdom would shake out.

John's expectations began to mess with his head. *Where is Jesus when I need Him? Where is this kingdom He was going to establish? Why hasn't He raised a battalion to spring me from this pit? Could I have baptized the wrong man? Is this Jesus really the true Messiah?* So from his prison cell, John sent word to Jesus: "Are you the one who was to come, or should we expect someone else?" (Matt. 11:3).

John the Baptist was not a man of wavering faith, but he was human just like the rest of us. No doubt he had his moments when things didn't turn out as he expected. I think this passage reveals him having a moment. Matthew Henry's commentary on Matthew 11:1-6 concurs:

> Christ appeared not in that external pomp and power in which it was expected he should appear; his own disciples stumbled at this, and perhaps John did so. . . . John's doubt might

arise from his own present circumstances. He was a prisoner, and might be tempted to think, if Jesus be indeed the Messiah, whence is it that I, his friend and forerunner, am brought into this trouble, and am left to be so long in it, and he never looks after me, never visits me, nor sends to me, enquires not after me, does nothing either to sweeten my imprisonment or hasten my enlargement? Doubtless there was a good reason why our Lord Jesus did not go to John in prison, lest there should seem to have been a compact between them: but John construed it into a neglect, and it was perhaps a shock to his faith in Christ.[1]

John's question was honest, but not faithless. Circumstances in this new kingdom of God had become so unlike what he expected that he needed reassurance.

Jesus' response was forthright and true: "Go back and

---

[1] Matthew Henry, *Matthew Henry's Commentary on the Whole Bible: Volume V—Matthew to John* (McLean, Virginia: MacDonald Publishing Company, n.d.), p. 148.

report to John what you hear and see: The blind receive sight, the lame walk, those who have leprosy are cured, the deaf hear, the dead are raised, and the good news is preached to the poor" (Matt. 11:4–5). In other words, *John, look past your limited expectations. Use your "kingdom eyes" to see the deeper truth. The kingdom is not about pomp and glory. It's not about gaining clout with which to squash the Pharisees and rout the Romans. It's about loving people into heaven.*

But Jesus doesn't stop there; He finishes with a strong word about offense: "Blessed is he who is not offended because of Me" (Matt. 11:6 NKJV).

It is reassuring to me that Jesus did not condemn John for his "moment." In fact, after sending the messengers back to John, Jesus turned to His disciples and paid the man a tremendous honor. I love how He said it: "I tell you the truth: Among those born of women there has not risen anyone greater than John the Baptist. . . . He is the Elijah who was to come" (Matt. 11:11, 14).

We tend to take circumstances and run them through the grid of our reasoning and then make our own judgments. We then decide if those circumstances are appropriate. In Jesus' own life—in this instance when He could have been offended at this question from someone who'd known Him since childhood—He chose grace and compassion. Through Him, we see that being offended is not what God intends as our first resort. Our first responsibility in new or challenging circumstances is to listen to the Holy Spirit and line up our opinions and judgments with our eternal plumb line—the very Word of God. His Word should be what guides our thoughts, our opinions, our responses.

GETTING BACK TO WORSHIP

Here is where we circle back to the subject of worship. Worship happens when we connect our heart with the heart of God. This means that worship rightly entails all of who we are. While we can't separate our worship from the essence of who we are—our character, attitudes, standards, and opinions—we can choose to rectify any convictions we have wrongly held. The question is: are we willing?

Those judgments, opinions, and even religious beliefs

that may have been innocently planted in our hearts could be the very things blocking a truly free life of worship. So we need to test our thinking, particularly when we're feeling offended at the packaging or the delivery style. Maybe we have bumped up against a truth we need to acknowledge.

I'm talking about sifting through the soil of our belief systems where early patterning or personal tastes have focused us on the surface instead of the true spiritual substance. We need to dig up those entrenched expectations that are so quickly offended and test them with the Word, asking the Holy Spirit to reveal the root of truth to us. I have a feeling that if we dropped our defenses before God's throne, our offenses would go away.

Some of my own misguided paradigms were born of great intentions. Still, well-intended but faulty belief systems are *faulty* nonetheless. And they subtly steal our victory as effectively as any identity thief.

How can we help the gospel to grow more fully and more alive in us, regardless of our personal preferences and opinions? We can be a people who stand strong on the

Word of God while refusing to take offense when others lose their footing. This corresponds directly with one of Paul's definitions of worship (and one of my favorites): "Therefore, I urge you, brethren, by the mercies of God, to present your bodies a living and holy sacrifice, acceptable to God, which is your spiritual service of worship" (Rom. 12:1 NASB).

When we become *living sacrifices*, that means no stone is unturnable in our lives. Everything must die so that Christ may live in us. That includes every paradigm and opinion and judgment we carry. We either fall in line with the Word or we don't. And worship in its truest form is exemplified when we bear the fruit of a life completely yielded to Christ's directives, not our own.

FACE-TO-FACE WITH OUR CHOICE

Look again at John the Baptist's question: "Are you the one, or should we look for another?" I wonder how often we ask the same question. You may not have realized that you've asked it because it sounded so different when it came out of your mouth . . .

- Is your church going to agree with me, or will you insist on being wrong and "force" me to go elsewhere?

- Is the worship you lead going to sound like I think it should, or does one of us need to leave?

- God, are You going to change my circumstances, or am I just going to have to turn away from You for not fixing this?

Entrenched expectations that are easily offended have no place in the life of a Christ-follower. When we come face-to-face with those places in us that need change, we have two choices. We can stomp off in anger and stubbornly build a wall that lets in only those who agree with us. Or we can humbly take those challenges to the Word and make needed adjustments, followed by those ridiculously difficult words that "the Fonz" could hardly force himself to say: "I was WRONG."

When we do the latter, we can repent and move forward. Forward is good.

I love John the Baptist's story. It gives me such hope! Like most worship leaders, I have this ego-stimulating, artsy, moody side to deal with. And when it gets the upper hand, it seems to hang a sign on me that says, "All Offenses Welcome Here!"

In my saner moments, I realize that being artsy is no excuse to extend my quills like a touchy porcupine. It's no excuse for letting my expectations dictate my responses either. If anything, this artsy nature should open a multitude of opportunities for God to grow me as a worship leader. Every challenge to my expectations can become an opportunity to show the graceful nature of God—an opportunity to choose *not* to take offense.

How amazing would it be if we all chose to keep our every belief, bent, and understanding captive to the Word! How appealing would the kingdom of God be to the lost if we did as Jesus did? If we sacrificed personal offense on the altar of grace and truth? If we offered to God a willingness toward short accounts? If we opened our hearts and minds to see Him as He is . . . not simply as we think He should be?

That would be a sweet, sweet sound in His ear.

5

THE WIDE, WIDE WORLD OF WORSHIP

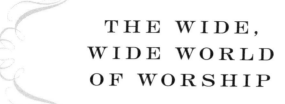

paradigm (n.) *a patterned way of thinking; a theoretical framework by which generalizations are formed*

After my eye-opening, youthful encounter with my legalistic attitudes, it'd be nice to say that my religious life was, like Mary Poppins, practically perfect in every way.

Not.

I still have a lot to learn about the true meaning of worship and the broad ways in which it can be experienced and expressed. Thankfully, I took a giant step in that regard over a dozen years ago when Angela and I joined a tour group to Israel. The group was composed of Christians whose ministries were in the arts. There were singers, songwriters, and worship pastors, dancers, writers, actors, painters, a sculptor, and even a figure skater among us.

At the time I had given little thought to the relationship between Christianity and the arts apart from music. What was the point? After all, it seemed to me that in the Bible, the arts as a whole didn't fare very well.

There was that golden calf Aaron had sculptors make, which pointed Israel away from God. There were all those lewd, idolatrous statues in Canaan that God demanded His people destroy, not to mention those ancient Greek actors who gave us the term "hypocrite." And dancing? Well, Salome's infamous, provocative dance was answer enough, wasn't it? Add to that everything the movie *Footloose* taught us about the evils of dancing, and to me it was "discussion over"!

Music must be God's favorite art, I reasoned. Why else would He apparently designate it as the one through which we worship?

Did I ever have a lot to learn.

My limited frame of reference had never exposed me to anything except my own denominational worship experience. And for us Baptists, music had always been the way we expressed our worship to God.

Now, I'm not degrading that experience because, for the most part, it was very positive. And I didn't feel anything was missing. I was just so musically bent that I couldn't imagine anything *but* music being one's go-to for expressing worship. I simply hadn't seen the bigger picture; I was perfectly comfortable sitting in my own little box.

Until this visit to the Holy Land. The change came through a single incident on that trip to Israel.

SEEING THROUGH STAINED GLASS

Angela and I met some amazing people and made some lifelong friends on that trip. Some of them became like family to us. (I think change comes easier when you're exposed to it through people you know and love.)

Of course, I was deeply moved simply by being in the Holy Land. Everywhere I turned there was some place or artifact that took my breath away because of its significance to me as a believer in Jesus Christ. The Jordan River, where He was baptized. The hill of the crucifixion. The tomb from which He was resurrected. It was awe-inspiring just to be in the same places Jesus had been.

Those of you who have been to the Holy Land know that many of those sites now have churches on them, built as monuments to the holiness of the events that occurred there. On one particular day, our tour group found ourselves in another of these old churches. Most of us were quietly strolling the grounds and absorbing the ambience. I stopped to observe the colors and design of one of the stained-glass windows, and thought to myself, *That's pretty*. But after a moment I realized I was not alone. Turning to my left, I saw a woman from our group standing beside me, a highly gifted visual artist whose paintings, drawings, and collages expressed a deep faith through a profound merging of the intellect and spirit.

As we stood almost shoulder-to-shoulder looking at that stained-glass window, I was surprised to see tears streaming down her cheeks. I knew immediately what was happening: clearly, the beauty at which she was gazing was moving her into the presence of God. Through that window, this woman was experiencing what I experience when I hear a song that moves me.

She was worshiping.

At that moment a long-shut door in my heart was kicked open. Suddenly I realized that my lame adjective "pretty" was utterly inadequate to describe what she was glimpsing in the magnificent windows of that church. The multihued light filtering through the stained shards of glass were beams of God's glory, shaped into inspiring forms and colors by the creativity of a gifted artist. The art in those panels could lead souls to worship the God who inspired it—and it was leading my friend, before my very eyes.

Were there other arts besides music through which people could worship? The joy on this woman's face gave me the answer—a resounding *yes*!

DIFFERENT WAYS, SAME MEANING

In that moment God changed my paradigm about what worship means. Each of us is His unique creation, moved in a way different from everybody else. We express our worship depending on the bent or talent God has given us.

While we all have a mandate to keep our worship biblical, God calls us to worship Him with the gifts He gives us. Like a kid who asks his dad for money to buy a

Father's Day gift, we can't give anything to God that He didn't first give to us. He is not going to give us something that is out of bounds. That means whatever gifts He gives us are the ones we must offer back to Him.

My gift is music; therefore I offer back to God the gift of song. But it was pretty presumptuous of me to think that the way I worship was the only way anyone *should* worship. Right there in that church, standing next to that visual artist who was weeping with joy at the sight of windows created long ago by another artist—an artist showing his adoration of God—it all came crashing down on me. I began to see that a painter worships as he paints, and his use of form and color and texture draws people to a Creator. A dancer worships as she dances, and her graceful movements inspire audiences to behold the divine Choreographer. The actor worships when he offers his craft to God. And the writer praises her Redeemer through eloquent words.

When I think back, I wonder why all this hit me as a surprise. It's not as if God had hidden the fact that worship can occur through other arts. Psalm 149:3 says, "Let them praise his name with dancing." Moses writes of two gifted artists, Bezalel and Oholiab, who were filled with the Spirit so they could create all kinds of beautiful objects for the Lord's tabernacle (Exod. 31:1–11). Then there are the gorgeous renderings of the Song of Solomon and the worshipful poetry of the Psalms. And what about the book of Job, which many scholars believe was written as a drama to be performed?

Above them all stands Solomon's Temple, a masterpiece of architecture and craftsmanship designed explicitly to express the glory of God. It was said to be one of the great wonders of the ancient world.

When that temple was finished, the Israelites came together for a massive dedication ceremony. The celebratory worship was in full swing when suddenly the presence of God filled the temple in the form of a cloud, transforming worship to awe as the people were overwhelmed by God's glory (2 Chron. 5). If the God of heaven descending into this man-made temple was not an endorsement of all the arts involved in its construction and celebration—architecture, sculpture, metalwork, goldsmithing, weaving, poetry, music, and no doubt many others—then I don't know what *endorsement* means.

A GREATER VISION

I was only in my mid-twenties when this worship surprise occurred, and I had no idea what God had in store for me. I had not yet started my ministry with Beth Moore. I didn't know that shortly after this trip I would be called to lead people in worship. But looking back, I can see that in that church in Jerusalem, God was giving me a new vision— perhaps similar in a small way to what He gave the apostle Peter regarding his perspective about the gospel.

Peter had assumed that the gospel was meant only for the Jews. God showed him a rooftop vision—a huge sheet filled with all kinds of "unclean" animals that Jews were forbidden to eat. Peter was hungry, so God invited him to choose his dinner from the selection. Peter had never eaten anything impure or unclean, and he wasn't about to start now. But the voice from heaven told him, "Do not call anything impure that God has made clean" (Acts 10:15).

What God was teaching Peter had to do with more

than just food. Jews—God's chosen people—thought all Gentiles were unclean and inferior. In the Jewish mind, the Gentiles were unreligious pagans. So when God sent Peter to baptize Cornelius, a Roman, Peter got the point. This Gentile was no more unclean than the animals God had offered him for dinner, which meant that God's saving work was much wider than the narrow, national salvation the Jews had envisioned.

Before placing me in a ministry of worship, God wanted me to likewise learn that worship is far more beautiful and diverse than this one-dimensional, cocky little redneck from the mountains of North Carolina had ever thought. Through that artist beholding that stained glass in Jerusalem, God opened my eyes and heart to the fact that the tapestry of His people is multicolored and vastly rich—well beyond my own experience or expressions. Not everyone is going to worship like I do—nor should they.

That was quite a surprise for this young punk. But it was one that I am thankful for. And it is one that I am mindful of to this day, every time I seek to lead His people in worship.

6

WORDS, WOUNDS, AND WORSHIP

heal (v.) *to make sound, healthy, or whole; to restore to an original or favorable condition*

I still remember the first time someone made fun of me in public: I was in the fifth grade. I remember where I was sitting. I remember what the room looked like: the lights were off, but the bright sunlight shone through the windows and lit up the far corners of the large, square classroom. I remember the words exactly: they were spoken by a classmate, and they were about me.

I remember how nonchalantly those words rolled off the kid's tongue. I remember the other kids laughing, and how their laughter seemed to signify a knowing, as if there was some longstanding inside joke and I was the only one excluded from it. The spoken words brought the sting. But being excluded from what everyone else knew inflicted the deepest wound.

It was as if that day marked the official opening of a construction site in my heart. The machines and crew came in. Signs and fences went up. Workers brought shovels and broke ground. And in that moment, a wall was constructed around my heart.

I have spent much of my life since then positioning my emotional defenses on the ramparts of that wall, guarding the wound that was created that day. To prevent being wounded like that again, I chose not to trust people. I went on the offensive in relationships, and I hurt people first— for fear that if I didn't, they would hurt me. Now, at age forty, I am—with God's help—unlearning those self-protective mechanisms that barricaded my heart nearly thirty years ago.

All because of words.

MORE THAN THEY SEEM

Words in themselves are just sounds—aural interpretations of vibrations in the air. But put those sounds together into a language, and they are a powerful force for both good and evil. The words of Churchill rallied Britain to heroic valor that saved his nation, while the words of Hitler incited a nation to commit unthinkable horrors and draw the world into war.

Through words we can be encouraged, thanked, built up, and inspired. But one tiny word can also wreck us, causing our ability to think and function rationally to fly out the window.

Not one hurtful thing about me that hit my ear ever left my mind. That's the impact of words. It's as if anyone's mouth had the power to hold my emotions hostage.

I'm guessing that you have also experienced the damaging force of words. Who hasn't?

Oh, the powerful tongue. James understood the destruction words can leave in their wake when he wrote:

> Take ships as an example. Although they are so large and are driven by strong winds, they are steered by a very small rudder wherever the pilot wants to go. Likewise the tongue is a small

part of the body, but it makes great boasts. Consider what a great forest is set on fire by a small spark. The tongue also is a fire, a world of evil among the parts of the body. It corrupts the whole person, sets the whole course of his life on fire, and is itself set on fire by hell. (James 3:4–6)

Come on, James. Don't pull any punches or mince words. Tell us what you really think!

James used strong words to describe the tongue because he understood just how powerful words are. In another verse, God goes so far as to tell us that "death and life are in the power of the tongue" (Prov. 18:21 NKJV). Our words will carry one or the other: life or death. If we don't constantly train ourselves to speak life, then we will speak death by default.

So here's the question: how can we lift up our lives as an offering of worship when we feel so wounded by someone else's words that we're afraid to even lift a finger? Unfortunately, the answer is *not* in our first inclination—which is to build a wall around our hearts. If we let these walls stand, our hearts may become impervious to hurt, but they will also become so hardened that they're impervious to love. We will isolate ourselves from others and from the joy that comes through relationships. That includes our relationship with God.

We can't close our hearts to others and expect to remain open to God. Wall ourselves off from relationships with people, and we will wall ourselves off from worship. The two are *that* connected.

OPTIONS, OPTIONS

So there you have one non-answer—what not to do. But the question remains: what can we do when words wound us severely?

I see two answers to that question, and the first may surprise you.

When we are wounded by words, our first reaction—aside from the hurt itself—is likely to be disbelief. Our heart will react defensively: "I can't believe he said that about me! How could anyone be so mean? How could anyone think that? I'm not like that at all." But keep in mind: we are fallen beings, and our hearts cannot be trusted. The heart is deceitfully wicked above all things (Jer. 17:9). That means we must stifle our natural defensive reactions—even our denial—and ask ourselves, "Could there be some reason he or she would say such a thing?" Chuck Swindoll says, "Your critics rarely hit the bull's-eye, but they seldom miss the target altogether."

So we must measure those hurtful words by God's Word. Take the insult, complaint, jeer, or ridicule to the Lord and ask Him: "Is there any truth in what was said of me?" This is hard to do, because we don't like being honest with ourselves in scrutinizing our faults. Most of us have developed either a willing blindness that doesn't see or a talent for self-justification that excuses our persistent sins. But we must learn to be ruthlessly honest in our self-appraisal. And if we find any truth in those hurtful words that were dumped on us, we must confess our discovery to God.

Did someone call you proud? Confess your pride. Ask God to humble you. "If we confess our sins, he is faithful and just and will forgive us our sins and purify us from all unrighteousness" (1 John 1:9). You might even thank God for using this person to bring you to a place of humility.

As for the garbage that is spewed on you in spite or envy, with no basis in truth, lay it down before God and let Him do the cleanup. Pour out your complaint to Him, knowing that His justice will prevail over those who falsely malign you (Psa. 63:9–11).

We can fight the power of false words with the power of God's words. The Lord empowers us to live above the evil that is said of us. As Paul put it, "I care very little if I am judged by you or by any human court; indeed, I do not even judge myself. My conscience is clear. . . . It is the Lord who judges me. . . . He will bring to light what is hidden in darkness and will expose the motives of men's hearts. At that time each will receive his praise from God" (1 Cor. 4:3–5). So renounce the curses spoken over you. Renounce them in the name of Jesus, firm in the truth that God's Word trumps man's words every time.

That's how you can know that you're not a loser: because God's Word says you're not. We are told that we are "more than conquerors through him who loved us"

(Rom. 8:37). No matter how we may be devalued by the words of others, we actually have enormous value because God thought we were worth the price of His Son's blood. "In him we have redemption through his blood, the forgiveness of sins, in accordance with the riches of God's grace" (Eph. 1:7).

Even as adults, we may still be bearing the pain of hurtful words spoken long ago. I did. I lived inside that well-constructed wall of self-imposed isolation, locked away from any chance of freedom in Christ. And the emotional wound simply festered. More importantly, as long as I remained behind such a wall, I was in a death trap.

If we truly have the faith to believe that we are who God says we are, we can step out of that trap—even in the midst of our fear—and into God's freedom. As Psalm 119:45 puts it, we can "walk . . . in freedom" because we trust the precepts of God's Word. It's simply a matter of common sense: if we believe what God says about us in His Word, then hurtful words meant to degrade us are just not true. That means we can throw out those words, and replace the hole they dug in our hearts with what is true.

It's a tough thing. Relationships can be a beast. And what makes it harder is that *relationship* is what we are made for.

HEALING, PART TWO

The next part of the healing process is not easy: you are called to bless the one who wounded you. I know, this is painful. But through the power of the Holy Spirit, it can be done. And it must be done as a necessary part of your healing.

So speak a blessing over that person. Ask God to forgive him. Ask God to work in her life to bring about His purposes. As the Spirit moves to soften your heart, go even farther. Pray for that person's family to be blessed. Pray for his finances. Her influence. As we yield to God's way of doing things, He gives us power—to the point that we can actually find ourselves praying for the person who hurt us as if we were praying for ourselves.

If I can do this, you can too. Pray aloud. Pray Scripture. The Holy Spirit will help you.

And the surprise in all of this?

Here is a hidden place of worship.
It is intimate and sweet.
Few find it.
But you can.

TURNING THE MIRROR
ON OURSELVES

So far we've talked only of pain inflicted on us by the words of others. But what about our own words? Are they always pure, uplifting, affirming, positive, and honest? Have you got that wild flapper in your mouth tamed to the point that it never does harm? I'm pretty sure that, like me, you've said words that harmed others. Perhaps intentionally sometimes, or in the heat of anger, but at other times unintentionally—maybe not even knowing you had inflicted injury.

I can remember one of the worst times I ever did such a thing. The story is so painful that as I type, I am debating with myself about whether to tell it at all. But I lost the debate, so here goes.

We Southerners often use the word "ugly" as slang for

being unkind, ill-natured, or unpleasant. I grew up hearing and using the word in that way. So as a parent, I thought nothing about it.

"Jack, don't be ugly to that boy. Please share your things."

"Lily Kate, let's not be ugly to Mommy. We need to have happy-to-do-it attitudes."

Angela and I said it as freely and innocently as any word.

One day the four of us (Levi hadn't been born yet) were all in the car. Lily Kate looked up at her gorgeous mom and said, "Mommy, you are so beautiful."

Angela responded, "Oh, thank you, Lily Kate! Thank you! You are very beautiful too, the most beautiful little girl in the whole world!"

"No, I not," Lily Kate answered.

Her reply sent shock waves through us. For me, it was as if someone had struck a blow to my chest. For that brief moment, I wanted to be swallowed up by the earth forever. I couldn't take it. My little girl—the one around whose pinkie I was securely wrapped, the one I knew to be the

most beautiful girl ever to breathe the air of this world—
did not think she was beautiful. How could this be?

Instantly, the Holy Spirit spoke to Angela. She realized that maybe our way of using the word "ugly" had been
misunderstood by our precious daughter. In being told not
to *act* ugly, Lily Kate was in danger of thinking that *she* was
ugly.

It was not an irreparable situation, and we did take
steps to mend things with our daughter. But the incident
taught Angela and me to be much more sensitive to the
power of the tongue and to more carefully choose our
words.

AS LONG AS THERE ARE PEOPLE . . .

As long as we live in relationships with people, we will deal
with wounds. Sometimes others will hurt us; sometimes
we will hurt others. But those wounds need to be repaired,
and that brings me to the next step in the healing process.

I said earlier that blessing the person who has hurt
you is painful. I'm afraid that this next step is even more so.
When we hurt another person—or even sometimes when

they have hurt us—we are called on to take positive steps to mend the relationship. Yes, this means more than blessing or praying. It means dealing with that person face-to-face and working out the hurt between the two of you.

Silence causes wounds to grow and fester. On the other hand, reaching out to the offender or the person you've offended can accomplish reconciliation and restoration. The key is to take care that we do it with words filtered through the sieve of the Word of God and spoken with the love of the Holy Spirit.

Now we are reaching the heart of why this chapter on words is in this book on worship. It is impossible to worship God while you are at odds with a brother or sister. The apostle John, known as the apostle of love, wrote, "If anyone says, 'I love God,' yet hates his brother, he is a liar. For anyone who does not love his brother, whom he has seen, cannot love God, whom he has not seen. And he has given us this command: Whoever loves God must also love his brother" (1 John 4:20–21).

This Scripture passage makes it obvious: you cannot close yourself off from a brother or sister in Christ and yet claim to love God. Our love for God is demonstrated and expressed in the way we love others. That is why Christ Himself said, "Therefore, if you are offering your gift at the altar and there remember that your brother has something against you, leave your gift there in front of the altar. First go and be reconciled to your brother; then come and offer your gift" (Matt. 5:23–24).

It couldn't be clearer, could it? Don't even try to worship until you have reconciled with your brother or sister. Until you take that step, your worship to God is a sham.

But what if you can't reconcile? What if you try and your brother or sister refuses? Or what if the offense involves people you can't contact? Does that mean you are forever cut off from worship? No, of course not. We are never responsible for how others respond. But we are responsible for how we respond. That is within our control.

THE FELLOWSHIP OF SUFFERING

Time passed, and I lost touch with the person who wounded me in my childhood. So that hurt stayed with me for a long while. I finally got to the point where I had to hold that wound up to God and say, "This *still* hurts. It renders me emotionally immobile. It scares me. What if I get hurt again? What if the joke is still on me?" Yet even in the midst of that pain, I pressed through by God's grace and worshiped anyway. And I found that the power of a life surrendered to God trumps the power the enemy tried to wield through that wound.

Now that wound is gone. Praise the Lord! It left a scar, but it's a scar that I treasure. It reminds me that I needed a healing. I needed a Healer. And He delivered.

Reconciliation won't always be successful, but we must make the effort. It's the most effective route to real healing and unencumbered worship.

Don't say you can't do it, because I know you can. If I can do it, you can too. No, it's not easy, but what does *easy* have to do with anything? Sometimes we are called to do painful things. Even to suffer. It's part of being a Christian.

We don't suffer to earn our salvation—Christ suffered once for all (1 Pet. 3:18)—but we understand that we're most like Him when we choose to forgive those who have hurt us and seek to reconcile with them. As we are told,

"Can two walk together, except they be agreed?" (Amos 3:3 KJV). There's a place of agreement between God and ourselves when we walk with Christ in forgiveness. This brings a deep appreciation for our own forgiveness and the great salvation we have.

Do this hard thing and you will find the healing ointment of Christ going deep into the wound and restoring it to health. As you bless those who have cursed you, you are identifying with the very nature of Christ. You are identifying with His sufferings. And that brings you into fellowship with Him. It's that fellowship that brings us to . . . *worship*.

Surprise.

7

FEAR. NOT.

abandon **(v.)** *to hand over completely and unconditionally to*
another's control; a full-fledged yielding

Yep. She's mine, and I'm raising her. We call her Lily Kate. She has my blood surging through her veins, but in her it's supercharged. Sometimes I look at this beautiful little creature and think to myself, *Where in the world did you come from?*

Like that time on a ride with some friends at Disneyland. You know the one, that weird elevator called the Tower of Terror. As you wait in line, you get this eerie build-up to the ride with video and holographic narrative. Images of Rod Serling tell the tale of a group of people who stepped into the fateful elevator and entered . . . *The Twilight Zone.*

Hey, I'm a grown man, and none of this affects me. I know what they're doing. The whole purpose of these elaborate effects is to get you so worked up that by the time you step into the elevator, your imagination will make you feel more of a thrill than the ride really provides. *I can see right through their scheme. I'm not about to get all excited about riding an elevator.*

Then comes the elevator itself. Our group steps on, and we are told to strap ourselves in. *More psychology. They're trying to make us think this thing could really be dangerous.* The ride attendants are ominous and kind of creepy. We buckle up, and then we wait for a moment. *Oh, no. My psyche has bought into this whole mess. I'm a little scared. No, I'm a lot scared.*

Suddenly the elevator drops like a stone into a well. It goes into free fall, building up something close to mach speed, and I feel my stomach pressing against my tonsils. We drop more stories than I thought the building had.

Just when I am sure something must have gone wrong and the elevator is about to crash into the bottom of the shaft, it slows abruptly, creating enough G-force to compress my six-foot frame to about four foot eight. My stomach is now pressing against my bladder. *Maybe I should have worn a pair of Depends.* I feel myself being shot back up to the top story again. And then back down. And up again.

I feel like a yo-yo on steroids. My eyes dart about in panic, looking for some way to get off this thing. An emergency cord or an abort button. *Somebody HELP!*

There's nothing. I'm trapped! I hear someone scream in utter terror. *Oh, wait a minute. That was me.* But it doesn't matter because everyone else is screaming too.

Everyone except Lily Kate.

She's laughing, her arms stretched straight up in sheer exuberance. I know, because at the worst moment of this near-death experience, those sadistic Disney people have the gall to snap a photo of us. Probably intended for blackmail. When I see the photo later, I don't look as bad as I feared. In fact, I am laughing. No one need ever know it was the maniacal laugh of temporary insanity intended to cover up my utterly freaked-out terror.

But not Lily Kate. She jumped into the moment with

her whole self, her laugh obviously real. Sheer joy. You can tell by the ear-to-ear stretch of her happy mouth compressing her eyes into little slits and the full-on, skyward thrust of both arms. She looks like a Spirit-filled worshiper at a Pentecostal praise service.

That's Lily Kate. That's the way that girl lives. All the time. She uses that God-given exuberance to take in every experience, to enjoy whatever the moment offers. Everything is exciting to her. You might say she is constantly on full tilt.

I'll have to admit that sometimes her zest wears me out. Sometimes it exasperates me. Sometimes it even makes me envious. But mostly it makes me love her so much it hurts.

And, it makes me want to live like that.

I want to plunge into every experience as if it were a breathtaking adventure. I want to trust God in every moment—even those fearful moments when it seems that the bottom has dropped out and I'm plunging into a void with no way to break the fall. I want to trust Him in those moments when the situation is completely outside my control. When it seems that the forces of evil have me in their grip, and there's no way out.

LIVING WITH ABANDON

Daniel 3 tells us of three young Hebrew men who had exactly that kind of trust in God. You know their story; it's always been a favorite of Sunday school teachers. These three men—Shadrach, Meshach, and Abednego—were condemned by the Babylonian king, Nebuchadnezzar, to be thrown into a blazing furnace for failing to worship Neb's new ninety-foot statue of himself.

Furious as he was, the king offered them a second chance before he turned on the heat. "But if you refuse," he warned, "you will be thrown immediately into the blazing furnace. And then what god will be able to rescue you from my power?" (v. 15 NLT).

I love how these guys answered:

> O Nebuchadnezzar, we do not need to defend
> ourselves before you. If we are thrown into the
> blazing furnace, the God whom we serve is able

to save us. He will rescue us from your power, Your Majesty. But even if he doesn't, we want to make it clear to you, Your Majesty, that we will never serve your gods or worship the gold statue you have set up (vv. 16–18 NLT).

Now, that's what I call trust. "Bring it on, O mighty monarch! You can't hurt us! We serve a God who will take care of us no matter what happens. We're sure of it. If we don't walk out alive, we'll be taken up to Him. Either way, we'll be rescued from your fire. Nothing you can throw at us matters in the least."

With that kind of attitude, I can't imagine these young men approaching that oven door with trepidation. I suspect "anticipation of adventure" was more like it: "Hey guys, do you realize what we're about to get to do? Either we're about to see what no man has seen before—what fire looks like from the inside—or we're about to see our God face-to-face."

They were headed for the time of their life, even if it was the time of their death. It reminds me of something

G. K. Chesterton once said: "Courage is almost a contradiction in terms. It means a strong desire to live taking the form of readiness to die."

You know the rest of the story. The guys' trust in God was not misplaced. Inside that fire they met an angel of the Lord, who led them on a casual stroll, kicking up sparks in those flames like a kid splashing in the surf. Then, when the king saw that Shadrach, Meshach, and Abednego were apparently noncombustible, he commanded that the door be opened, and out walked the trio unharmed—not a singed eyebrow hair. Not even a hint of smoke.

Whatever those young men may have felt going in, I think I'm safe in guessing what they felt coming out. Elation. Excitement. Passion. I figure they must have been at least as elated as Lily Kate on the Tower of Terror.

EVERYTHING COULD CHANGE

Can you imagine what your life would be like if you had that kind of trust? Think of how it would change things. How it would change *everything*. No more fear. No more worry. All the downer events that we Christians call "trials" would become adventures. Instead of facing those moments with anxiety, we could face the unknown in anticipation: "I wonder what kind of surprise God has up His sleeve for me this time?"

The psalmist wrote, "God is our refuge and strength, a very present help in trouble. Therefore we will not fear" (Psa. 46:1–2 NKJV). We can be oblivious to danger only when we trust in the Savior. We don't have to know what lies beyond the elevator door. We can say with confidence, "Lord, I don't know how this is going to turn out, but I do know that You are with me. So I don't need to worry about the outcome. And if I don't need to worry, that frees me to accept whatever comes my way as an adventure."

Think how this would change your outlook. Your attitude. Your capacity for joy.

Trials will come into your life—you can't help it; you can't prevent them. But you can help how you face them. You can prevent them from killing your joy. You hold the power . . . when you give the power over to God.

Christians who throw themselves into life with complete trust can face life with real zest. That *savoir-faire* atti-

tude toward life will spur us to sheer joy when we encounter the unexpected.

We read that after Peter and the apostles had been
arrested by the Jewish leaders for preaching the gospel,
they "left the high council *rejoicing* that God had counted
them worthy to suffer disgrace for the name of Jesus" (Acts
5:41 NLT, emphasis mine). Their adversity was a cause, not
for worry but for worship.

And Paul was just like them. That irrepressible, ener-
getic, fearless champion of Christ encountered fearful circumstances everywhere he went. Yet he may have been the
most joyful Christian who ever lived. From one of many
prison cells he wrote, "Rejoice in the Lord always: and
again I say, Rejoice" (Phil. 4:4 KJV).

If he had this kind of joy on a bad day, what must he
have been like on his good days? Paul and his rejoicing. I
would be angry at him if he weren't so right.

The Christian life to these heroes was nothing less
than an adventure. The greater the danger, the greater
their trust. And the greater their trust, the greater their joy.
That's what inspired them to worship wherever they

were—in prison cells, on trial before a hostile jury, or in the roaring blast of a furnace.

TRUST, WHATEVER COMES

Today I think most of us are inspired to worship when God's blessings are of the obvious kind. Good health. Plenty to eat. A roof over our head. A reasonably hefty bank account. A good car to drive. A good church. Good sermons. Good worship music. No squalling kids in the audience. *God is good! Let's praise Him!*

Okay, it's true that God's abundant blessings are a worthwhile cause for praise. I never want to be ungrateful for what He's given me. But I've come to suspect that to have the kind of joy those three Hebrew boys had, the kind that Peter and Paul had, I've got to have their kind of trust in God. Not trust that He will make my life easy and pain-free, but trust that whatever comes my way, I can rely on Him to hold me safe. To pick me up. To keep me in His care.

Deep down inside, that's what I really want. I want the kind of trust that knows He will bear me up when it seems the ride is in free fall. I want to feel complete confidence that whatever happens, I am safe in His arms.

When I look back at the snapshots of my life—those that were taken in my most fearful moments—I want to see my hands thrust toward the sky, my head thrown back, and a mile-wide smile stretching my face and squinting my eyes into joyful slits. I want to live my life just like Lily Kate lives every day.

Whatever may come, I trust You, Lord. Bring on the adventure!

THE GREAT
ADVENTURE

adventure (n.) *an unusual and often exciting undertaking that may entail unknown risks; a remarkable experience*

Most of my ministry has been of a traveling kind, and I love it. As a hopeless sanguine, I love meeting all kinds of people in all of the places I've been fortunate enough to go. I love the food, the cities, the churches, the friends. Yet I've always kind of thought that at some point, if the traveling ended, I might eventually be blessed to serve as a worship pastor at a church.

However, as I stared my fortieth birthday in the face, I had never felt even the slightest urge or calling to end my traveling ministry (and still haven't). Furthermore, after watching some of my worship-pastor friends go through really tough circumstances at their churches, I pretty much vowed (an unholy vow, mind you) that the chances of my ever joining a church staff were zero. Why would I want the hassle? When I looked at all of the wonderful things God had called me to do—writing, arranging, leading worship, traveling, and touring—there was no sense in complicating this perfect picture with a church position. So I just assumed I would stay on this current train with Jesus and ride it off into the sunset.

But assumptions are never safe.

The unraveling started when my team and I were in the final weekend of our *Jesus Saves Live* tour. It was a Friday in November of 2009 at a great church in Jackson, Tennessee. At the end of the concert, the pastor came onstage. You know the scene—that typical, pastor-handshake-while-everyone-claps moment. He thanked us graciously, closed the concert, and left. Truthfully, I don't think I even looked that guy in the eye.

Later, when everything was packed and loaded, I climbed on the bus and said the strangest thing to my team: "I think I could grow old with that pastor." I don't know what possessed me to say it. I had never met the man, never had a conversation with him. In fact, I was convinced that there was no pastor or church that would have me. But something about this guy quickened my heart. Hard to explain.

I had watched as he worshiped with his wife during the concert. They whispered to each other, prayed together, raised their hearts in surrender together. I had heard a little about him. His name was Ben, and he had been a pastor for only three years. Though he was young, for some inexplicable reason I had an innate trust in him.

I didn't think anything more about Pastor Ben until two weeks later, when he called to ask if I would lead the worship for his church's women's retreat the following year. We had closed our booking for the year, but his vision resonated with my spirit, so Angela and I decided to accept the invitation. Since Angela's parents live in Jackson, we would consider it a work-vacation weekend. The kids could ride horses and four-wheelers with their grandparents while Angela and I led at the conference.

A couple of weeks later Ben called again. His worship leader had resigned. Would I help him find a replacement?

Sure. I knew many great guys in worship ministry; I could connect him with several who would fit his church.

Ben wanted to visit face-to-face about the church's needs, so he drove the two hours to my home in Franklin to meet with me. I was prepared with a list of six or seven people and my assessment of each.

When he arrived he explained what he was looking for and how it fit his vision for his church. We quickly developed a close rapport, which led the conversation down all kinds of rabbit trails. I kept steering the conversation back to worship pastors, but I was puzzled that he seemed uninterested. I finally made it through the list and asked him what he thought of my candidates.

"Travis, just forget your list," he said. "I'm not interested. I actually came to your house today because the Lord put *you* on my heart as the guy for this church."

I practically laughed Ben out of my house. I told him I wouldn't even consider it. My family's future was set. This Cottrell train was moving along nicely and wasn't about to switch tracks.

Ben's offer was very accommodating: I could keep

doing what I was doing and just make his church my home base. I would have a staff to make it all happen; they'd arrange things so the church wouldn't miss a beat when I was away. But I didn't budge one inch.

To me, it was the equivalent of moving to Jupiter.

TAKING INVENTORY

Ben and I had become friends, so we continued to text and tweet after he returned home. He was still convinced that I might be his man, and yielding to his persistence, I did promise to pray about it. I'll admit that his conviction caused me to feel a slight pressure on my heart, but I charged it to my regret at having to disappoint him. I was happy where I was, so I continued to give Ben a moderately defiant *no way*.

On Sunday, December 20, I was traveling between Raleigh and Louisville when I got a text from Pastor Ben saying (as I recall it):

I've been on my prayer bench, and God will not release your name from my heart. Will you please respect the fact that I feel that I'm hearing from God on this, and at least open your heart to pray about it? If you feel that God still gives you a "no," I promise to leave you alone and never mention it again.

His words made me realize that although I had prayed about Ben's offer, I hadn't really opened my heart to it. So on that Sunday, I tried to do just that. It bugged me that as I prayed, the pressure I had earlier felt on my heart increased. A lot. When I told Angela about it, she figured it was just one of those midlife guy things: "Oh, sweetie. You're turning forty. Bless your heart, it'll be okay. Do you need a new car or something?"

That all changed as I drove my family to Boone, North Carolina, for Christmas. On that snowy day driving across Tennessee, Angela and I unpacked everything about our lives together—dreams realized and unrealized; God's definition of success in ministry; God's standards for walking uprightly in the kingdom; how to fit our kids for their callings; and what needed to stay or go in our lives so that

God could freely use us as equippers in the body of Christ. We pulled out every aspect of our lives—the good, the bad, and the ugly—and looked at it in the light.

There is something fulfilling about putting on the brakes and taking a full-scale, life inventory—but it's also very dangerous. Convinced that we had opened ourselves to the will of God, Angela and I began to pray. And pray hard.

"Lord," I said, "You know I will go *anywhere* You call me. And—"

At that moment God interrupted me in my spirit. "Now just hold on right there, Travis. That is not true."

Suddenly I realized that it wasn't true. I had closed myself off from certain kinds of callings. I had decided what my path would be, and I was already on it. God didn't need to speak to me: my mind was made up.

Obviously, God had some work to do in me. In both Angela and me. And the process began on that trip to Boone. We asked Him to get our hearts where they needed to be—completely open to His will. We put ourselves on the chopping block in a way we had never done before.

This was a deep work, plumbing the depths of everything we were, and it was exhilarating. And scary.

During this time, God took me to Isaiah 33:6—a verse that would wave over us like a banner in the coming weeks: "He will be the sure foundation for your times, a rich store of salvation and wisdom and knowledge; the fear of the LORD is the key to this treasure."

This verse kicked us into higher gear in seeking God's plan for our lives. We needed the wisdom and knowledge of which it spoke to direct our future. We needed the foundational assurance that if we were open to God, He would secure our lives. We even needed that fear of the Lord to alert us when we were not as open as we pretended to be.

Openness to God is not as easy as it seems. It means dying to our own plans and allowing Him to point the way. Deep down I wanted to do that, but how did I know where He would point? I didn't. And that was a problem. (It still is sometimes.)

Throughout Christmas, both Angela and I wrestled like Jacob with God to find our way to His true will for us. We would sometimes awaken at night with a deep sadness or in a state of panic. When we went to the Lord, these feelings would subside.

I still didn't think God was leading us to a worship ministry with a church, and I still didn't want it. Mostly, I thought all this internal turmoil was simply about the Lord growing us in areas where we needed maturity, not about picking us up and moving us to a far-away country like Jackson. Or Jupiter. (At that point, living anywhere else might as well have been Jupiter.) Yet if we were truly going to be open, I realized we had to put the possibility of Jackson on the table.

Angela and I gritted our teeth, opened our hands and our hearts, and truly put ourselves out there to the Lord. And a strange thing happened. Our hearts began to make a turn. Not a sudden turn; it felt more like a huge ship laboriously turning around. As the turn was happening in our hearts, the thought of refusing this call to Jackson began to feel more painful than the thought of leaving Franklin. All of which compelled me to listen more closely to this call.

But a tinge of fear still lodged in my heart. I wasn't afraid of losing my present ministry—Pastor Ben had embraced it wholeheartedly. And I wasn't afraid that God would give me a task I hated—He tells us in Psalm 16:6 that our boundaries fall in pleasant places, so I trusted Him to give me joy in whatever He led me to do. And I had no fear of the job itself—so much of the work appealed to the things that I've always held so dearly about music ministry: pastoring a choir, leading a team of worship leaders, guiding college kids through their transitional years, investing in a community, and dreaming of crazy-brave things to do for the glory of God with a pastor whom I love.

The more I thought, the better it looked.

A YEAR TO REMEMBER

Obviously the ship was slowly turning, but being open to God doesn't come easily for us fallen humans with our built-in will. I was trying hard, but little tentacles of fear still gripped my heart. I was a mess of tangled uncertainty.

Finally, Angela and I decided to get together with Ben and his wife, Lynley, for a "get to know you" visit. They left their kids with grandparents and arrived at our house on New Year's Eve. After a fun night of games and eating and ringing in the new year, Ben and I stayed up until 3:30 talking about ministry, vision, and a bunch of "what ifs." We got on our knees and prayed for God to make Himself clear.

The next morning as we all ate breakfast, Ben jumped in with questions for Angela about her thoughts on the possible move, and she didn't hesitate to return the fire. As the morning ended, I was greatly conflicted. I was happy that the four of us had talked openly about possibilities and dreams. And I was happy that Angela seemed to have a light spirit about it. But fear still gnawed at me. So many questions and obstacles kept looming up that the chance of us moving seemed minimal at best. On the other hand, I had already begun to dream of leading the people in Jackson. So with all these conflicting dreams and fears, I was feeling pretty down. Sullen.

Ben and Lynley planned to leave around noon, have lunch at the local mall, and do a little shopping before they headed back to Jackson. We decided to follow and join them for lunch. But first, Angela and I asked if we could pray for them. We huddled up in our den while our kids lined up on the couch, taking it all in.

That's when it happened. The miracle. The surprise.

We prayed. We prayed for twenty minutes. And as we poured out our hearts, the Holy Spirit descended into our den. It was a moment so intense and so filled with power that I want to talk about it, yet it was so sacred that I could never convey the fullness of its impact. It will ring in my spirit as one of the most profound moments of my life.

Our kids sat quietly on the couch for the entire twenty minutes (a miracle in itself). And with that prayer God began to knit our souls together with Ben and Lynley's. The Lord had started a work, and now all four of us were on the same page about it.

WHAT NEXT?

After the prayer the four of us hugged each other awkwardly, so stunned by the huge God-moment that we didn't know how to walk away from it. So we did what anybody would do: we headed to the mall food court.

As we got in our car, I looked at Angela, awe still lingering on my face maybe a little like God's glory lingered on Moses. "What was THAT?" I exclaimed.

"We are in trouble," she replied. "Lord, have mercy. Lord, have mercy. LORD, HAVE MERCY!"

I wouldn't want anyone to misinterpret what Angela was saying. It was not a cry of despair or a call for rescue. It was almost the opposite—a recognition that suddenly our lives were in the hands of God, and our own will didn't amount to a hill of beans.

It was a cry of exhilaration, of surprise. It was acknowledgment of the fact that our exhausting time of introspection, culminating in that moment of prayer, had produced exactly the result we'd wanted. The result God always promises, but which sometimes seems so elusive. We had finally opened ourselves to God, and He had spoken into our lives in a most profound way. And now He was in control, not us.

It was scary, but it was a good scary—like waiting in line for a roller-coaster ride. Still, we had not made our decision. But then came one "coincidence" after another. I'll give you just three examples.

Angela was looking for something in an old journal, and when she opened it, these words in her own handwriting were staring her in the face: "Lord, thank You for bringing my family to Jackson."

Whaaat?

She just "happened" to open the journal in which she had taken notes at the Beth Moore *Living Proof Live* conference held in Jackson in November of 1999—ten years to the week before our concert at Englewood Church. She was thanking the Lord for bringing her family to that event.

Angela and I needed counsel. So we called our pastor, we called Beth, and we e-mailed our team of intercessors. They all committed to pray and to give us words as God directed. Immediately, two separate intercessors sent us the same scripture. Another "coincidence."

Then one evening, after a day of constant worry over this decision, I pulled up my comfy chair beside the fireplace, grabbed the TV remote, and went searching for something that would take my mind off of this nonsense. The movie *Walk the Line* was on.

Woo-hoo! I thought. *I'll soak up somebody else's hard life for a while; maybe it will give me some much-needed perspective.*

Within seconds after I tuned in, Johnny Cash (Joaquin Phoenix) stepped up to the microphone to sing. What did he sing, you ask?

"I'm Goin' to Jackson."

Come on, God. Is this for real? Is this how You're gonna play?

I do think God has fun messin' with us like that sometimes. He'll use anything from a sledgehammer to a funny "coincidence" to get our attention.

Once we put all those events together, Angela and I finally said it. We said what God was waiting to hear us say: "Yes. We get it. We give. We surrender. We raise the white flag. We're with You." And, in the words of good ol' Johnny, *"We're goin' to Jackson."*

ANOTHER BEND IN THE ROAD?

We had made our decision, but wise counselors advised us to wait for a period of time before giving Ben our answer. If our inner turmoil had caused us to misunderstand God, a waiting period of unpressured quiet would enable us to hear Him more clearly.

In the interim, we snuck over to Jackson to visit a Sunday service. Of course we were concerned about uprooting our kids, so we wanted to see their reaction to this church. They had a great morning; we had to drag them out of their Sunday School classes.

"Please, Daddy, can we move here?" they shouted as we navigated the halls.

"Shhhhh! Let's take that volume down a little, please," I said as I covered their Dr. Pepper-moustached mouths. "We'll talk about it later."

Another confirmation of our decision. The joy was too much. Too much.

The date we had set to give Ben an answer was February 3. But here in the middle of January we were already convinced. I held to my date, however, because the story of Abraham came to my mind. God seemed to have him on a definite path to sacrifice his son, Isaac. But at the last second God caught a ram in the thicket for him to sacrifice instead. Was God going to give me an eleventh-hour ram before we walked this offering through? Would He show us yet another bend in the road?

At times I felt like I was watching for God's hand with one eye open and one eye closed—all the while scared that He was sending a ram. At this point, I was connected enough to this new call that I would've been heartbroken at the sight of a ram. But no further word came, and on February 2, Angela and I felt total peace about the decision. So at 12:01 a.m. on February 3, I called Pastor Ben.

"Hey," he said.

"No ram in the thicket," I replied.

True peace and joy flooded our souls. And celebration ensued.

FOREVER CHANGED

In spite of the sense of closure, there was still one last thing to be done.

Now it was up to the Lord to move through the hearts—and votes—of the people at Englewood Church. I led worship at Englewood on Valentine's Sunday, and one week later the members voted. Angela and I were fully submitted to their authority and ready to accept whatever they decided.

As we waited for the decision, I thought back on this arduous journey with gratitude and reflected on how my life with the Lord had been forever changed. Because of all He walked me through in this adventure, I no longer feared much of anything anymore. He had shown Himself to be so faithful, how could I doubt His ways? I could honestly say that God is so big and so in control that if the church voted no, I would passionately pursue Him just the same.

Going through this process also reminded me of a surprising thing about worship. Worship consists of submitting to God and His will in every facet of your life, and then loving and praising Him whatever the outcome. I love the chills and thrills of musical worship, but there is another music that sings in my soul when I am aligned with God. To find that alignment doesn't always come easily. Sometimes it's painful. Sometimes it's through the fire. Sometimes it's wading through my own small (and sometimes not-so-small) disobediences. And sometimes it's through the desert of change. But when I released my fear in true submission, I found a song of worship singing in my soul. And it rings there even now.

WAKING TO A NEW DAY

Well, the votes have been counted, and I'm happy to say . . . cue the music, Mr. Cash . . . we're goin' to Jackson.

Surprise.

Today is a new day. And it's a good day to open yourself up to the voice of God and invite Him to speak to you in ways He never has before.

Is He calling you into a great unknown? Is He calling you to a new form of service? Is He asking for more surrender than you've ever given Him? Whatever your situation may be, I'm pretty sure He is working to help you see yourself and your calling like He sees it, and not within the confines of your own experiences and wishes.

I guarantee that when you open up to God's view, you'll be surprised at the joy and freedom your worship at the altar of surrender will bring.

I know. I'm basking in His joy as we speak.

SURVIVING
DEATH

comfort (v.) *to offer hope, strength, or support in a trying time;*
to ease another's grief or trouble with consoling words or deeds

Last week I attended three funerals. Three different people,
all in different stages of life, coming from three very different circles of friends, and dying in the midst of three very
different circumstances.

None of them died of natural causes.

The more I think about that phrase "natural causes,"
the more it bothers me. I have come to realize that there
is nothing natural about death. It's hard to take, hard to
understand.

Even for Christians who do "understand"—intellectu-
ally, at least—death is awkward, bringing questions beyond
our ability to answer. We grapple with how to handle the

loss of people who are dear to us. We want desperately to figure out God's role in it. And sometimes, when grieving people hit us with these questions, we feel a need to cover for God, as if He let something happen that He shouldn't have.

Of course, we know that death was not God's idea; He never wanted it to happen in the first place. In fact, the apostle Paul calls death God's enemy (1 Cor. 15:25–26).

We are the ones who invited death into God's perfect world. Yet when we lose a loved one, we tend to fall back into thinking that God, being all-powerful, should have done something about it.

Well, He has. He went so far as to endure death, along with great pain and anguish, in order to get rid of death for all eternity. But until eternity arrives, we still have to deal with it.

MEMORIES OF MY MOTHER

Since my mother passed away six years ago, I have never been able to attend a funeral without thinking of her funeral. There's a knowing that is adopted in your spirit once you are one of the "front row few" at a funeral. It's not the best seat in the house, that's for sure.

As long as I can remember, Mom had been sick. Although her illnesses were serious, she refused to let them keep her from being active.

She was an avid golfer, seldom missing Ladies' Day at the Boone Golf Course. She also kept the books for my dad's business. We're talking old-school bookkeeping, with a typewriter, carbon paper, and hand-addressed invoice envelopes.

Mom's most renowned legacy was created in her kitchen, where she turned ordinary foods into works of art. But everything in Ollie Jean Cottrell's busy life gave way to being a mom to four kids.

Some people thought it should have been only three kids. And I believe it would have been only three had there not been something about that generation, about the kind of family she was born into, and about the faith they held to be all-important.

They were part of that "greatest generation"—hardworking, God-loving, faith-affirming survivors. Ollie Jean was the youngest of nine children, born to farmers John and Leannah Wilson in 1930. They passed on to her the value of never leaving a job unfinished or a need unmet and the principle that right was always right and wrong was always wrong.

When Mom became pregnant with me, she was thirty-nine, and she already had three children—a boy and two girls ranging from seventeen to twelve. She had just survived thyroid cancer, lost an ovary to cancer, had a tumor in her uterus, and was on birth control. It's a miracle that I was even conceived.

When the family learned of the pregnancy, they were naturally shocked, but they were also excited. The doctors, on the other hand, were highly concerned. Because of my mom's age and many health issues, they warned that her life was at risk and urged her to abort. She refused. Abortion simply was not in her vocabulary.

By God's grace, everything went well with my birth and delivery. Of course, my parents were older than most parents of kids my age. They may have felt sheepish or embarrassed when people asked if I was their grandson, but I absolutely loved the fact that they were older. In many ways, it was like having parents and grandparents all in one. Having already raised three kids, Mom was in the stage of life where she didn't have a whole lot to prove. She had overcome a young mother's anxieties and fears and developed the laid-back, tender spirit of a grandmother. A grandmother who wasn't easily ruffled by a whiny little boy. Being the son of older parents taught me a lot. It shaped who I am. I am grateful.

As Mom got older, though, she began to battle other illnesses: emphysema, high blood pressure, osteoporosis, and a fierce case of arthritis and gout. A few years before her death, the arthritis slowly disintegrated the bones in her neck, putting pressure on her spinal cord. This produced a severe curvature of the spine, which pushed her head forward and down toward her chest. For the last two years of her life, she could not lift her chin off of her breastbone.

It was really tough to see her like this. Mom was an elegant "head held high" kind of gal, both literally and figuratively. Even though she may have been embarrassed at the effects of her illness, she had that inner steel that made her just as elegant and beautiful then as she had been when in perfect health.

As Mom's condition deteriorated, we knew her time was short. Angela and I were serving at a *Living Proof Live* event with Beth Moore in Lexington, Kentucky, when my sister called, saying that Mom apparently had only a few hours to live. I remember that Beth's topic was *El Olam*, the Everlasting God. She shared letters from people who were dealing with the loss of loved ones. Beth's teaching did much to prepare us for what we expected to soon face. But after a few days in the hospital, Mom improved and returned home.

Several times in the coming months she was back in the hospital, and each time we got that call again: "Come home. Mom seems to be at the end." But after a stay in the hospital she would rally. I learned later that my brother and sisters often sang one of Mom's favorite songs, "I Love You, Lord," over and over to her on those nights when her pain was unbearable. That song seemed to give her more comfort than the strongest pain medicine the doctors could administer.

But one night, I got the final call. It was on August 25 at one o'clock in the morning. Mom was with Jesus.

I awoke Angela and we cried together. After making plans to leave for Boone, Angela went back to sleep. I couldn't sleep, so I sat down to do the one thing that remained in wrapping up my work on a new CD, *Alive Forever*: I wrote my thank yous—and a new album dedication.

> I would like to dedicate this project to my dad, Glenn Cottrell, and in memory of my mom, Jean Cottrell, who went to be with Jesus on August 25, 2004. Mom, I will never sing "Alive Forever Amen" the same again. I will always be thinking of you and how you are in the presence of your Redeemer. How complete you must feel to be in His presence. Dance away on those golden streets, Mom! Enjoy your new healthy body! We miss you, but you are where you were made for. And we were made to be there, too we'll see you soon. Until then, you are in my heart forever.[1]

---

[1] From the CD liner notes of *Alive Forever*, Travis Cottrell. © 2004 Integrity's Hosanna! Music.

Since I had selected the songs for this CD entirely at random, I had not realized until that night that the entire collection was a personal testimony of the resurrection power of God. It was a fitting soundtrack for what was happening in my personal life.

God used this CD to comfort me with the truth that my mom was *alive* and in the presence of Christ. Even in my grief, I could celebrate her homecoming.

> *Let my heart sing out*
> *For Christ the One and Only*
> *So powerful and holy rescued me*
> *Death won't hurt me now*
> *Because He has redeemed me*
> *No grave will ever keep me*
> *From my King*
> *I'm alive forever amen*[2]

---

[2] "Alive Forever, Amen." Words and music by Travis Cottrell, David Moffitt and Sue C. Smith. © 2003 First Hand Revelation Music (admin. by Ministry Copyright Services)/ASCAP, Integrity's Hosanna! Music/ASCAP and New Spring Publishing, Inc./CCTB Music (both admin. by Brentwood-Benson Music Publishing, Inc.)/ASCAP.

A PLACE OF COMFORT

The family gathered in Boone to share our grief and celebrate Jean Cottrell's triumphant life. After our private family visitation at the funeral home, my dad gave each of the grandchildren stationery on which to write my mom a letter. That afternoon Angela and I, my siblings and their spouses, and all the grandchildren put pen to paper to articulate the love we had for Jean Cottrell. We then placed them all inside a drawer in her casket.

Angela wrote a letter in her journal that simply thanked Mom for raising her son the way she had and for being a good mother-in-law. She closed her note by saying she was thankful that the sickness and pain were no longer present, and that Mom was healed and leaping with her Lord like a deer on the high places.

Mom's funeral was tender, emotional, and sweet. At the end of the service, all the grandkids lined up in the front of the sanctuary and sang the song that had comforted Mom the most during her sickest days. It was very hard for those heartbroken kids to sing "I Love You, Lord." But even through the tears that sometimes made their voices waver and break, this song brought exactly the comfort and release needed by everyone there who dearly loved Ollie Jean.

It occurred to me later that the most comforting moments since my mother's death were those in which I praised God. When Beth spoke of the comfort of *El Olam*, I praised Him. When I realized my CD inadvertently and repeatedly celebrated the Resurrection, I praised Him. When I learned of Mom's comfort at being sung her favorite song in the hospital, I praised Him. With my letter for Mom's casket, I praised Him.

In a way, it seems a strange and surprising thing that in the moments of our deepest grief and emotional pain, it's worship that brings the best comfort.

Think about it: my family and I were experiencing the loss of someone we loved dearly. This side of eternity, we would never again see or hug my mom, enjoy her company, or lay eyes on her beloved face. And yet, we praised the almighty God who, with a flick of His little finger, could easily have turned a miracle that would have healed this person and restored her health. Instead of blaming Him for letting her die, we sang "I Love You, Lord." We worshiped, and in worship we found comfort.

How do we make sense of this oddity? I think one of the best starting points is in Luke 24, where two deeply grieving disciples met a stranger on their way home from Jerusalem. The stranger joined them in their walk and asked why they were so downcast. They recounted the death of Jesus, whom they had hoped would redeem Israel. But Jesus had been executed, and though there were rumors of His resurrection, they had seen no evidence of it.

The stranger explained that Jesus had to die and be resurrected before redemption could be accomplished. When the pair reached their home, they invited the stranger in for dinner. As they ate, their traveling companion revealed Himself as the resurrected Christ and then disappeared, leaving them with an afterglow of utter elation.

Now *that's* a surprise.

Two things comforted these disciples, turning their grief into wild joy: an understanding of the Resurrection, and the presence of Jesus. These are the very things that comfort us in our grief.

ALIVE FOREVER

First, the Resurrection assures us that death is temporary. As much as God hates death, He loved us so much that He willingly experienced it so that, by His resurrection, He could bring us out of the grave and into eternal life.

Just as Jesus had to die in order to defeat death through His resurrection, we also must die in order to shed this sin-contaminated body and be resurrected to perfection. That is why we cannot demand that God prevent our deaths. The pain is terrible, but pain is necessary to produce the glory. As Beth Moore often says, the goal of life is not the absence of pain. And I believe that to be true. The goal of life is the glory of God. In joy. And yes, in pain.

Ecclesiastes 3:11 also assures us that while we cannot fathom God's purposes from beginning to end, "he has made everything beautiful in its time." That's a truth we can rest our lives on.

Second, we are comforted by His living presence, which we receive by the power of the Holy Spirit through worship. Jesus' living presence assures us of the truth of the Resurrection, validating His promise to resurrect us.

Therefore, as Paul tells us, we do not "grieve like the rest of men, who have no hope. We believe that Jesus died and rose again and so we believe that God will bring with Jesus those who have fallen asleep in him" (1 Thess. 4:13–14).

For those of us who have accepted God's gift of life through His Son Jesus, even grief in its rawest and most palpable state cannot help but be laced with hope. This doesn't mean that death no longer hurts. It hurts terribly. Sometimes the pain of our loss seems so devastating that we wonder if we'll ever recover. But our hope is in *El Olam*—the Everlasting God. Our God who saved us, frees us, and holds us is eternal. And because He shares eternity with us, we don't weep as those who are without hope. We worship the One who has firmly "set eternity in our hearts" (Eccl. 3:11).

Take that in. His Word tells us that we are made for *eternity*. This is why death is so repulsive to us. We hate it; we resist it; it tears us apart. Why? Because we were not made for death. It insidiously invades our existence, but it is not the final event.

In Beth's teaching on *El Olam*, she said: "Our bodies

are subject to time. But our hearts are subject to eternity. And hence the conflict every day that we live. We have something inside us that says *life was meant to be forever!* And we're right. Because it is. Forever. Forever."[3]

On the day of Mom's funeral, after the services had ended, Angela and I were walking with my sister Vickie up her long, wooded driveway. Suddenly a huge, strong buck with a beautiful rack of antlers leapt across the driveway right in front of us. It took our breath away. It was as if the Lord was reaching out to us in our time of grief and saying, "My beloved is here with me. We are running together in the high places. And she is finally free!"

It was a beautiful surprise.

[3] Beth Moore, "Names of God" (*Living Proof Live* event presentation, Lexington, Kentucky, August 2004). © 2004 Living Proof Ministries. Used by permission.

SURRENDER

surrender (v.) *to cease resisting another power; to yield to a different influence*

As I sit on the other side of the worship adventures I have recounted in this book, I recall those man-made boundaries I once placed around worship. Then I reflect on the surprises that have forced me to rethink the meaning of worship and how I can adjust my thoughts, practices, and conclusions accordingly. Obviously, the old definitions I once held were entirely too narrow. To think that worship entails only the hour spent in a church sanctuary each week is like thinking Sunday lunch is the only meal I need to nourish me for the week.

The stories in this book tell only a few of the many lessons I've learned on my journey toward understanding worship. Some have been easy, some painful. Some funny, some brutal. Some of them I've shared; others I will hold quietly. But there are a few big lessons that stand out above the others because they continue to wave over my life like a banner. Lessons that are key to walking in freedom, power, and peace.

Some lessons seem to be more veiled. Others are clearer, like these. As I close this book, I want to leave these three discoveries with you.

1. There is always something next with God.

You may be in a season of life where things seem questionable; maybe they even seem desolate . . . hopeless . . . over. Your circumstances may be trying to dictate to you that God has not come through, nor will He.

But guess what? Not only are those things untrue, but the real truth is actually the opposite. And if you will free up God to be Lord of your life, giving Him your surrender, He will give you beauty for your ashes and strength for your weakness. And He will turn things around more quickly than you can say *Mayday*.

Mary Magdalene's life was as hopeless as any you'll find. Seven demonic spirits had taken over her body, and she was trapped in a bleak future. "Mayday!" Jesus came and pulled her out of despair, casting the demons from her. And the Gospels show clearly that from that moment on, she surrendered her life to Him. She was one of the few who followed Jesus regularly (Luke 8:2). She was one of only four people who stood by Him at His crucifixion (John 19:24–26). She was the first to see Jesus after His resurrection (Mark 16:9), and the first to announce His resurrection to the disciples (John 20:18). This woman with a hopeless past submitted herself fully to the Lord, and He blessed her with the power to live a new life—and with the honor of being the first to witness and proclaim the greatest event in history.

Hers is just one of many biblical accounts that reminds us: if we could only see the spiritual realm surrounding us, we would know that God's help is available at all times, ready to meet our deepest needs and get our lives on track.

Truth is, it doesn't matter who you are or how messed-up your past. You have not been disqualified, overlooked, or undergifted. Your gifts (or lack thereof) are a non-factor. Your geography? Not a factor. Your past? Only gonna disrupt God's redemption if you let it.

But you know what really took me by surprise in all of this? The fact that there was something next for us with God, and I didn't even know we needed a "next." So, the question is not: is there a next? The question is: when will it come? Be sure that it will.

2. There is nothing God cannot do.

I'm a lifelong church boy. I know churchy stuff. Sad to say, I was "religious" before I really loved Jesus.

As you've read, I pretty much always knew *about* the Lord, but in those early years I didn't really know *Him*. I knew I needed direction; I knew there were things in my life that needed to change; and I knew that I needed a plan for my future. I should have relied on God for these things, because in my head I understood that there is nothing He cannot do. And I believed it. I could quote prominent scriptures about how He makes His power available to work in people's lives. Scriptures such as . . .

Jeremiah 33:3 *Call to me and I will answer you and tell you great and unsearchable things you do not know.*

Jeremiah 29:11 *"For I know the plans I have for you," declares the* LORD, *"plans to prosper you and not to harm you, plans to give you hope and a future."*

Zephaniah 3:17 *The* LORD *your God is with you, he is mighty to save.*

I had seen God do the impossible in other people's lives, and I had experienced His power in many ways. Yet somewhere deep in my soul there was a question about just how much I could expect God's power to work in my life. I guess I figured that some things were left pretty much up to me.

Paul tells us that we can ask God to enlighten the eyes of our hearts so that we can see Him and see *like* Him (Eph. 1:18). When I finally let go of my own plans and gave my life over to God, He did just that for me. He not only changed my heart, He changed my mind. Literally. He changed the makeup—the constitution—of my thoughts. He altered my dreams. He completely overhauled my understanding of my calling, my purpose, my hopes. I never saw it coming, but man, oh man! I am so thankful for what He did.

I thought I had my life figured out. I had drawn the blueprint myself; I had written the ending in my head. But God, by His grace, swept in and, with His unlimited power, reworked the entire structure of my life.

I would never have prescribed such a mind overhaul, but here I am, immersed in a sea of gratitude that has overwhelmed my life. There are many miracles interwoven in my story. But perhaps the greatest is that God took the heart of this stubborn, change-fearing guy and completely revamped it.

If God can do that for someone like me, then it's obviously true: there is nothing He cannot do.

3. There is a key to true worship.

You may be wondering, what do these things have to do with worship? Well, the answer lies in something I said at the beginning of this chapter.

I think we all have a basic understanding that worship means much more than just what we do in a church building on Sunday. The word itself comes from the Old English, and in its religious usage it means ascribing absolute and all-encompassing worth to God. To worship God is to offer Him what He is worthy of receiving. God is worthy of our adoration, love, and devotion because of the absoluteness of His goodness, love, and power.

That concept carries so many angles, so many images, that I tie my brain in knots thinking about it. Obviously, in this wider, more encompassing view of worship, what we do in church is only a tidbit of what it means. As the experiences related in this book show, worship comes in many forms and springs from many circumstances. We worship out of our need, our plenty, our joy, and our grief. We worship in the middle of disaster and when disaster is averted. We worship in our exuberance and in our anxiety, in our health and in our pain. We worship when our emotions are touched by profound music or great art. We can—and should—worship wherever we are and in whatever we're doing. We should offer to God what He is worthy of receiving.

All that is well and good, but it leaves me asking myself, "What can I offer that God is worthy of receiving? Am I offering anything that really matters?"

Now we're getting down to the nitty-gritty. Ultimately, there is only one thing we can offer God, and that offering is the essence of every act of worship. What is that one thing? Our selves. And that means surrender.

What do we mean by surrender? Consider a young girl named Mary in Luke 1. The angel Gabriel came to her with an astounding assignment: she had been chosen to give birth to the Son of God.

Before you jump to the conclusion that no woman would refuse so great an honor, consider the consequences. Mary, an unmarried virgin, would carry the stigma of bearing an illegitimate child for the rest of her life. Society would look down on her. Also, she no doubt assumed it would mean the loss of her fiancé, as well as any hope of marriage in the future. All eligible men would shun her as damaged goods.

A great honor? Yes. But at a frightful cost.

So how did Mary answer the angel? "I am the Lord's servant. May everything you have said about me come true" (v. 38 NLT).

Now that's what I call real surrender. She laid her reputation and her hope of domestic happiness on the line and allowed God to chart the direction of her life. And after making that decision, she did not bemoan her cruel fate or become a drama queen with a martyr complex. What did she do? She *worshiped*. In fact, verses 46 through 55 give us the worship song she composed in response to her surrender to God.

Worship doesn't depend on easy tasks, ideal circumstances, or perfect lives, but on a surrendered heart. Worship is saying to God, "You matter more than anything in my life. You are wiser than I am. You are purer and more powerful. I submit to what You are and what You are doing in my life. I trust You because You are God and I am not."

Even though I had been a professional worshiper for years, surrender was the lesson I still had to learn. I am a strong-willed man who likes control. Especially control over my own life. It was in that "goin' to Jackson" experience that I learned the truth about myself: I wanted to be god of my life. I wanted to follow the course *I* had set for myself.

When I surrendered my will to God—admitting that He is all-powerful and all-loving and that I could trust Him with the "next" He had for me—that's when I truly worshiped. I offered Him the only thing I really ever have to offer: myself. And that's when God moved mightily in my life.

I can't tell you how freeing that was. Suddenly I could let go of all those sleepless nights and worries. I could quit being concerned about my future. I could lay down all of my prewritten endings to every scenario. All that was now in God's hands. I could get on about the serious business of God's eternal glory in my life. And I was free.

HOW TO HAND IT OVER

Overall, I think the big surprise about worship is that we don't find God only where we think we should find Him (for many of us, that's within the walls of a church building). We must allow ourselves to look for God in every corner and under every rock in our lives—good, bad, or ugly.

As the stories in this book show, the key to finding and worshiping God has nothing to do with what circumstance we are in. The key is in what we do when we encounter Him. What we must do is surrender. True worship simply boils down to that.

How do you surrender? Seek the Lord. Immerse yourself in His Word. Submit yourself to good, godly teaching and counsel. Ask for prayer. Ask for help. Open your heart to the work of the Holy Spirit.

Hand over to God the blotched canvas of your life—with its failures, hurts, worries, misunderstandings, and insecurities—and let Him repaint it with the beautiful colors of redemption.

In the simple.

In the grandiose.

In the mundane.

In the pain.

In the serving.

In the giving.

And within the context of everything . . . in the surrender.

When we surrender, we might just find ourselves surprised that our offering has brought us where we belonged all along . . .

Worshiping at the feet of Jesus.

AVAILABLE NOW MUSIC BY TRAVIS COTTRELL

AN INCREDIBLE WORSHIP EXPERIENCE...

JESUS SAVES LIVE includes 12 glorious songs, fully orchestrated, and featuring a three-hundred voice choir of Woodstock Baptist Church. Travis Cottrell's friends and fans will find JESUS SAVES LIVE a beautifully woven collection of songs full of encouragement, beauty and truth.

CD: $14.99
UPC: 878207004325

THE EXPERIENCE CONTINUES...

One extraordinary evening of worship...
Seven thousand worshippers gathered together & three very special guests.

Live performance DVD features teaching from BETH MOORE and MAX LUCADO.

DVD: $14.99
UPC: 878207004394

FOR THE CHRISTMAS SEASON...

"Ring the Bells" features some well known classics and six newly recorded Christmas songs including an awe inspiring duet with GMA Female vocalists of the year, Natalie Grant on the title track "Ring The Bells."

CD: $14.99
UPC: 878207003427

MUSICAL EXPRESSION AND LYRICAL IMPACT...

Travis's first full artist record featuring the song "Your Word is Life to Me" from the Beth Moore Daniel Study. Found is a record of sweeping, cinematic proportions, a classical pop collection featuring the Prague Symphony Orchestra.

CD: $14.99
UPC: 878207000228

WWW.TRAVISCOTTRELL.COM | WWW.INCIITE.COM   (i)in:ciite

Share Your Thoughts

With the Author: Your comments will be forwarded to the author when you send them to *zauthor@zondervan.com*.

With Zondervan: Submit your review of this book by writing to *zreview@zondervan.com*.

Free Online Resources at
www.zondervan.com

Zondervan AuthorTracker: Be notified whenever your favorite authors publish new books, go on tour, or post an update about what's happening in their lives at www.zondervan.com/authortracker.

Daily Bible Verses and Devotions: Enrich your life with daily Bible verses or devotions that help you start every morning focused on God. Visit www.zondervan.com/newsletters.

Free Email Publications: Sign up for newsletters on Christian living, academic resources, church ministry, fiction, children's resources, and more. Visit www.zondervan.com/newsletters.

Zondervan Bible Search: Find and compare Bible passages in a variety of translations at www.zondervanbiblesearch.com.

Other Benefits: Register yourself to receive online benefits like coupons and special offers, or to participate in research.

ZONDERVAN®

ZONDERVAN.com/
AUTHORTRACKER
follow your favorite authors